MULTIVERSE

MULTIVERSE

New and Selected poems

Tzveta Sofronieva

*English translations and originals by the poet
and with translations by Chantal Wright*

Edited by Jennifer Kwon Dobbs

White Pine Press / Buffalo, New York

White Pine Press
P.O. Box 236   Buffalo, New York 14201
www.whitepine.org

Acknowledgments of the original sources are listed on page 257.

Cover image: "Without title 14." Ink on paper. Copyright © 2016, Mária Chilf

First edition.

Printed and bound in the United States of America.

ISBN: 978-1-945680-37-3

Library of Congress Number: 2019944708

MULTIVERSE

CONTENTS

INTERSECTION GRAPH

UNLOST IN TRANSLATION

TRAJECTORIES AND LATITUDES

THREE TIMES DAILY RHINOCEROS BICORNIS

ANTHROPOSCENE

WONDER DETECTOR

INTRODUCTION

Jennifer Kwon Dobbs

Tzveta Sofronieva is a multilingual poet, trained as a physicist and philosopher of science. Born in Sofia, Bulgaria, and residing in Berlin, Germany, since 1992 Sofronieva grew up fluent in Bulgarian and English while coming of age in the former People's Republic of Bulgaria. She earned a master's diploma in physics focusing on quantum mechanics and its history and a doctorate in philosophy on the transfer of scientific disciplines, for which she did extensive research in universities in North America. A Walter-Rathenau fellow at the Technical University of Berlin, she also completed postdoctoral research at the University of Cambridge, St. John's College.

Early in her thinking, she embraced a materialist approach to poetry and resisted the idea of borders between disciplines, languages, and peoples including its twinned idea of the poet serving as a bridge between cultures. Instead, as scholar and award-winning translator Chantal Wright notes, Sofronieva pursued a vision of poetry "preoccupied with the water under the bridge rather than with the bridge itself: with water as a feminist, non-territorial space; with water as language, water as literature."

These commitments to the materiality of spaces, to language and literature distinguish Sofronieva's extraordinary, prolific career spanning eighteen collections of poetry across four decades beginning with her debut poetry collection *Chicago Blues* (1992, bilingual edition, Bulgarian and English). Also an acclaimed translator, playwright, literary installation artist, fiction writer, essayist, editor, and anthologist, she has been translated into eleven languages and received international prizes for her writing—some of which include the Adelbert-von-Chamisso-Förderpreis (a prize given to German writers whose cultural background is not Germanic), a poetry award from the Bulgarian Academy of Sciences, the Cliff Becker Book Prize for *Eine Hand voll Wasser / A Hand Full of Water* translated by Chantal Wright, and the Max Kade Writer-in-Residence at MIT in Boston.

Multiverse: New and Selected Poems culls from this prodigious output—bringing together representative and recent poems from Bulgarian, English, and German (some of which have been edited for this edition or translated into English for the first time)—for a retrospective and invitation to one of Europe's most radically imaginative and innovative poets. Readers first encountering Sofronieva's work will have the impression that they are in the presence of a major voice, well-read and well-traveled, whose emotional resonance and command of languages and literary traditions are universal and intimate, alert to histories and myths, and grounded in a scientific and lyrical understanding of the spaces that we inhabit and that inhabit us. In this regard, long after the Revolutions of 1989 and their aftermath,

14

her poems today retain a freshness and urgency about the oppressive consequences of human arrogance manifesting as an authoritarian regime, capitalist violence, the climate crisis, nationalism, patriarchy, and war.

Sofronieva goes to the root of these horrors—the Cartesian ego—and writes against its presumption of space as an absence to fill with itself. She merges physics and poetry to reimagine and encounter space as the presence of a dynamic force of possibility. Written almost thirty-eight years ago, "I or Cloning" stages the poem as a chemical reaction and dream alchemy; a combustion of images releases a sensual lyricism that is uniquely the poet's own:

> The snow's breath
> is liquid nitrogen
> in the laboratory of the self.
> Over the cracked white vastness
> time snows in crystals.
> Quantum-question — quantum-silence,
> quantum-question — two quanta silence,
> splinters of I. Quanta are units of light
> as snowflakes are units of snow.

Sofronieva tracks in precise measurements the "splinters of I" as multiple selves, or clones (as the poet has referred to them), that enable a multiplicity of language-worlds—all existing simultaneously. The quanta released from this splintering illuminates through simile poetry's transferral of energy and interconnection. In Sofronieva's work, scholar Anne Sturm writes, "the transformation of the elements references the translatability of languages and experiences."

Translation and multilingualism give access to a multiverse in which language-worlds co-exist and hold together, attracted to each other's linguistic surfaces. In long poems, most notably the lyric sequence *Anthroposcene* originally published as a chapbook-length poem (Translingual Series, hochroth Bielefeld, 2017), Sofronieva writes with a dramatic sweep in the spaces among languages—playfully inventing new words from Albanian, Arabic, Basque, Bulgarian, English, French, German, Greek, guitar chords, Hungarian, Romanian, Serbian, Spanish, and musical notation—sometimes combining and recombining phonemes in associative patterns of sound and visual syntax.

The poem's title, itself, is a new word that she invented to signify "the present epoch (from the time of the first discussion on the Anthropocene and onwards), during which humanity has begun to be aware of its own self-performance." Among anthroposcene's eight meanings, its last one names the stakes for her translingual play's disruptions:

> 8 : a psychological state in which humans are obsessed with fears and in order to escape from them again believe themselves to be the center of the universe and the purpose of the world's creation; this does not prevent them from destroying more than creating. Provoked by anthropocentrism, an unscientific, religion and idealism related doctrine

To this hyperactive anxiety about the future that only reasserts the Cartesian ego and risks further environmental degradation, destruction, human displacement, exploitation, and violence, Sofronieva offers a twenty-first century vision of poetry in which the "splinters of I" are not fragments of the self that are lost as fallout in a waste-land's chaos, but rather the creation of a way of seeing whole worlds and a range of futures in motion. These worlds will continue to interact with each other, just as words and the particulates of words will interact and in unforeseen ways produce meanings anew.

But Sofronieva does not look for consolation in universal laws or seek an abstract sense of belonging for herself or her readers. Her radical poetic—marrying together environmental, geographic, linguistic, lit-erary, political and social contexts—insists on poetry as borderless and unbounded. Poet-scholar-translator Johanna Domokos writes of Sofronieva: "She has freed herself from the normative, self-censoring effect of the majority literary language policy and is experimenting with entirely new poetic techniques in the field of multilingual lyri-cism." The poet's senses are open and her attention fixed on the free movement of worlds, words, and people.

"There are no refugees anymore / We all can go back," she writes. We can all go back to our limitless creativity—our sense of play and wonder—without blindfolds, wizened by the twentieth century's ca-tastrophes, and conscious of our responsibilities that come with so much power. In the final poem ending *Multiverse*, she reminds that our finitude is both a limit and the gift of a categorical imperative. In our freedom, we must be accountable:

> We have bombs, energy, genetics,
> a multiverse of responsibilities.
> We have a lot of dangers
> that are our own fault

and others that are not.
We will not be here for long.
But we have unlimited sets of possibilities
to experience.

In the twenty-first century of human experience, poetry will continue
to look with awe at nature, but no longer as a mirror in which to con-
firm and track a single worldview along a teleological timeline. The
movements of nature splinter the glass, as they always have and will
continue to do, but in unexpected ways brought on by the new epoch.
Fearless and restless, Sofronieva is that rare gift of a poet who is a
guide out of the standard rehearsals. Leave the swamp glow of that
theater and go with her into the snowy night, lean toward the cold
heat and the shards, see their patterns, hear their tones, touch the
energy emanating from the shifting spaces between them, and with
Sofronieva leap into the multiverse.

I.
Hurricane in Mesembria

I or Cloning

I, I, I, I... only four times
and the word becomes totally senseless.
—Lars Gustafsson

Snow rushes towards me
asking questions,
encounters my silence.
Frost biting vapor awaits me,
burns my skin, sharpens my eyes.
The snow's breath is liquid nitrogen
in the laboratory of the self.
Over the cracked white vastness
time snows in crystals:
Quantum-question — quantum-silence,
quantum-question — two quanta silence,
splinters of I. Quanta are units of light
as snowflakes are units of snow.
My hair is ablaze with snowfall,
and nitrogen turns to love
in the crystal-melting hair.
The road wastes its breath
in persuading me to clear the snowdrifts.
The nitrogen has already vanished.
I, I, I or the snow and I?
The light is fixed.

Child

One cloud embraces another
as light flakes snow on sea shoulders.
White is fickle. Seagulls'
wings transform it into blue.

Endless sky, bottomless sea,
but only looking in the well
do I see the heavens
and believe their depth.

Sand fog hides the tentacles of sea animals.
Don't be afraid—they're no sharper
than other things. Doesn't the moon
look smooth only because it's so far away?

Stars sparkle without a tremor behind the atmosphere
searching air to confuse themselves.
A corner collects their rays
in the charm of a web, the spider

lends a hand to them for the long journey.
I have just started out
and forget to look up. Is it too early
to make my way on my own?

I am only a bat in a room
lit by a false light—
even a mayfly understands that.
The true light stings

and leaves the darkness alone.
Black is the light in its infinity
yet resplendent and vibrant.
My mother knits a pullover

with luminous threads that I tag.
A child draws hats over clouds,
over seagulls, the well,
and one over me.

Sunday Expectation

I used to hate Sundays.

I hated being needled through the eye of relationships—
all the time pricking myself with the pin
I sewed more out of good manners and boredom.

Grandma did not have it in mind to die.
She left it to me to find, in one day,
both the hearse and the white shroud.
She departed beautifully that Sunday.

I forgot her biblical words.
I forgot the jaws of death
gnashing false teeth.

What I remember are deliberate footsteps in the snow.
My blood stains every betrayal.
In my dreams I keep waiting
but Sunday never comes.

I didn't invent the rules. I don't even follow them.
My breath evaporates among the stars
and never comes back.

And I sit with the embroidery.

Birthday

The clock tower grumbled at noon,
no cake or ceremony, only autumn.
The beating rain washed the cathedral's columns
from the inside, then pooled in the corner;
I was already wet. The river—slow and turbid—
murmured with understanding. Touristic
pigeons, blatant and gullible, bit my sandals.
I was soaked, but felt no anger. I gasped for air
at each bend of the cathedral's endless stairs
until I saw a door at the top of the tower.
It led to my past, to time's cogs
and the mechanic measurement: Someone
was born. And God was among the ciphers,
but through the movement of the hands
the clockmaker smiled.

Graphic Novel in the 1980s

The lamps of the boulevard are octopi
poking me with dirty light, the shy
lanterns on the alley are mainly broken,
the long sweeping curve from the shimmering glow
of the popcorn machine, the boy's hair
smeared with lemon and sugar
from a lack of styling gel, his face
disappointed with the dullness
of Halley's Comet, on sale
shabby Women Day's tulips, a swollen
belly leads the next couple to the altar,
the pregnant bride might be in love,
a cellophane look dominates the cafés,
a pocket calculator, unfamiliar
in the milkman's hands, winter
wished it hadn't been born,
cold overdone fries wait for me at home,
and the sun will rise the next day
most likely the same.

Perestroika Beach Carnival
or The Great Salvation

The spiderwebs hid in the Black Sea
and are now a species of algae.
The children's sunglasses on the beach
compete for color with their shorts.
A loudspeaker invites us with thunder
to visit the carnival on Central Beach.
The sea smiles slowly. Foam after foam
washes ashore. Today it's white and clear.
No admix of beige from sand or spiders.
With white words the sea will at last reveal that secret.
Oh, what happiness to be here! To be present!
But we all know it's not enough. Last night we dreamed
the astonished faces of our dead grandmothers as children:
We are ready for the conversation.
The kids who disliked the sea now toddle in.
The kids who always liked it joyfully
bail clams and small fish out of the water.
The fathers swim far off.
All ladies learn not to sink at least.
Mothers and brave girls forget to grieve and look ahead.
The secret. The sea smiles in white slowly.
The waves rise and rise—bosom of a young mother.
Oh, isn't it time for the red, even for a black flag?
The lifeguards rush in—they will stop the sea
with their whistles. A female voice screams through
the loudspeaker: "It's absolutely forbidden to swim!

Absolutely forbidden to bathe!
Absolutely forbidden to enter the sea!
Absolutely forbidden!"
I enter the sea with the lifeguard.
It was easy before, and I waited on shore diligently
reading books. He condescends, permits me to wade
in the shallows. None of the children obey—
they throw colored things on the shore:
pants, shorts, and sunglasses. The adults,
mostly the mothers, stay in the water.
Lifesaving whistles whizz. OK! OK!
I too am forbidden. I remain blown by the foam—
oh, if only my knees could melt to a less sexy form.
But stop it! Enough! I am fed up with talking politics!
The lifeguard is apologizing—it was
an order from Central Beach for the sake of the children.
All lifeguards must answer to a superior lifeguard
helicopter, which roars more loudly than the sea.
Where does it land? It stinks of fuel and oil.
Oh sea, and you complained against sun oils?
The beach becomes deserted.
Did the tourists go, or did they resettle in the sea?
Ah, here they are, under the solar showers.
And the children with their grandmothers' faces
from last night's dream are looking in surprise at my knees.
Music. Pop music from all over around—what chatter!
The spiderwebs gnaw at the sea and entwine with it.

The Earth Protests

Earth longing for more affection
demands the freedom to love the ocean,
refuses the heavy burden of the houses
and swallows them up. Mad earth—
feels drawn to the farthest coasts, and more—
wants to merge with water
toward perfection, hurrying far away.
We hold the ocean back with dunes, yet
it isn't water that drags and rushes in.
The earth resents and solemnly pulls away.

Hurricane in Mesembria

Nesebar is exploding, the churches are crumbling,
and have long since forgotten to love the sea.
Seaweed waltzes on the windmill's paddles,
propels them faster than the wind.
The tourists hide in a nearby resort,
the beach is magnetized by its encounter,
sharks gnaw at the sand for their evening meal
and proclaim: The full moon has been postponed.
The moon hides under the veil of the storm
within dirty clouds of haze and crabs,
we pale in the swell of feelings,
even the old stones shift position.
Nesebar didn't wait to be swallowed by degrees,
threw itself into the sea.
We'll go on seeking clues in the sand
that point to meaning.

Snowdrops

I thought—
snowdrops grow only in this part of town.
The revolution begins in this very square
and in that one in the village
in front of my grandparents' house.
I was blonde and had both ribbons
and cherry earrings.

I placed a ribbon
            on Red Square—
so naive, so many burnt illusions,
            on the Acropolis—
what a play with the ancient, the forgotten one,
            in the halls of the Vienna Opera—
such snobbery, longing for Europe,
            and in the room of Anne Frank—
I met human war face to face.

I gave the earrings to enter the Niels Bohr Institute—
so many nights in the world of the unpredictable,
saw my poetry in the paintings of Chagall and Paul Klee,
heard politics from the love songs of Sade
and from many other modern love songs.

I didn't change my watch at Greenwich,
only my hair, and once again
in the street corners snowdrops have blossomed.

Journey to the West

—for Margaret Atwood

A word in an unknown language.
I know there must be sense,
must be a meaning.
It's probably marginal.
Maybe a preposition
or a noun.
Either used often or
too strange for the ear.
Learning all languages
I listen attentively
to the springs of their speech.
I follow the air in the circles
of the vowels coming to me
from mouths of people
close to me and far away;
search for a language in which
I am a word.
I am already acquainted with it. It's foreign.
I have no idea about its syntax and morphology.
Even after studying the grammar for a long time,
I do not appear in the right place in the sentence.
Foreign in my own language, too,
in the Bulgarian spoken on the streets of Sofia
and used in my mom's letters.
What a funny accident—right now,

history sits at my parents' tea table.
In Bulgaria words slowly acquire
their old meanings.

Sometimes

the wine is white and red and pink and purple if you love it
the streets are munich montreal paris and mars the moon you love
the men are black white and green and blue which you may love
women are blonde with colored eyes and brown lips for you to love
the year is gorbachev or bush or hussein or me and you who love
the day is first and last and work and fun and past and present
future days of love which could be yellow orange light or dark as
        you do love
the hours the moments full of snow and lakes and depth you loved
the flowers without scents in all my tongues there is no real word
for smells which constitute the worlds of love and gods and bodies
the smell is you the wind of fingers touching eyes the smell is time
the time a time sometimes timeless no time in time long time ago
a touch of time in a bottle of old wine french as you usually love it
the smell of life which never was inside hotels where people live
a smell of fresh young and loving branch of a tree across this street
the wine is green and brown and deep white red cold as you love it
green hair dark brown lips white lips cold soft lips melting in love
a drop of wine on warm wet lips green hair reflection in a glass
the streets are amsterdam new york istanbul sofia bangkok
vienna venice new orleans jazz these streets are jazz piano
played by old hands music full of smells of love of old silly love
naive idealistic love parents' love children's love of my love
the love of universe of piano sound

In Times of Rain

Poisoned umbrellas
fly instead of butterflies. Among
greenish houses, trees seem gray.
Cats and sparrows are drenched
in this hunt when phones are
the only link between friends.
Letters wash away. Damp,
fake and unreadable news.
We as targets. It's time
to wake up, shake a leg.
The cracking of our bones
will split the rain,
breaking the spell, and a passerby
will leave his umbrella at home.

In memory of Georgi Markov

Homesick

so much here is a reality show
tenderness mixed with pornography
Halloween is not sorrow for the dead
but horror thrillers a carnival of witches
this continent is a hyperactive
teenager on a supersonic motorbike
with thick dark glasses and earphones
tomatoes grow injected with hormones
firm as plastic and have no taste
chickens are flavored to be fat
life is in cars in popcorn in cinemas
in huge shopping malls where one
gets lost in music specially produced
to make people buy to consume life
as a big bouquet of artificial flowers
scrubbed every morning with too much
water and detergent

Premiere

The shimmering fish stays afloat,
gasps for air and glistens. There is no net,
no fisherman, no catch. The fish,
iridescent, trembles a bit
much as the dead tremble.
No, no, it's not resentful.
The ice was thick, the winter hard.
Pet fish quickly die from it.
The goldfish came from another land.

It is a golden fish
in the garden pond of a Central European landlord.

Interference Pattern

There are moments in time
when it pours in waves
and the picture becomes
distinct and clear:
captives, refugees, sects,
homeless, migrants, lonely ones.
But light ripens in our hearts
and brings brightness to the world.
It is the old age of darkness,
blind and dreaming,
not frantic but wise.
Is memory the aging of time?

Time superposes and interrupts
as a diffraction pattern of light.
Trapped in its interlaced outline
and afraid to talk quietly I scream.
I feel helpless with the pain of those
who search for paradise
and more helpless against water shortage.
Is there a superlative for helplessness?
I am the sieve that breaks the waves of time
and also the canvas on which they combine.

We are responsible for the long distance
from us to us, or you to me,
where time roams
until it self-destructs.

Colored Against Gray 1:0

It's the rats. The rats are the ones.
We tried to copy the colorful in color—
avoided black and white, the sad and ossified.
But the one who is destined to swallow gray after gray
runs into a rat—a big one, strong, hopping next to us—
how couldn't we notice it!
A grayish one, rather fat, almost the size of a rabbit,
ran behind the opera. They recognized it.

"Rakovska" exploded, the trolleycars screeched,
the lonely women howled like lionesses,
a desperate man waved his umbrella about.
The sixth-floor suicide sighed in relief
and decided against it—up there
he's at least far away from that blood.
And you pushed me to the opposite sidewalk,
so that we don't see
how indignant fellow citizens beat the animal to death
in the hope that red may color his gray body,
the gray cane, the gray sidewalk, the gray paving stones,
the gray buildings and skies.

And I thought we would find it,
the six-color copier in a copy shop behind the opera.
I believed and convinced you.
I'll have to sit in the bath for a long time
until the warm water
reddens my skin turned gray from Sofia's gloom.

An Evening before Bulgaria's
First Democratic Election

The men in parliament unbuckle their belts.
Oh, they are so smart!
I drink
as I have never done before.
And they are talk-ing all the time.
"-ing" as in the end of Boeing—
airplanes to transfer passengers overseas.
A talk. A drink. They talk. I drink.
A creature of the female gender
who learned many theories,
loves these childish men,
and returns from the States
to create something here,
I drink alcohol for the first time in my life.
And God, I do not like it.
I must drink to my courage in being here
and to celebrate my birthday.
An evening before a new government is delivered.
I do not want to get drunk.
I do not want this government either.
Life, children,
I want children
and life.
What are the lyrics of hell?
Dante?
My crazy drunken poem,

this depressing drivel—
who needs it anyway?
A communist Jew,
a perfect strategy for survival, told me:
"Dante writes about human passion
out of any social context.
Look what a context we have here!"
Oh God, let us survive.
I wish myself a future.
They push me out
to the States, to Canada, to heaven.
I dislike heaven. I dislike crises, saviors,
whatever and whomever.
I want to stay home.
I want life.
I want children.

We were not cavalry horses

1.
Never written letters ramble in my head.
Never received letters ramble in my heart.
My friends—spread out far away
and the spaces of silence between us,
spaces deprived of faith, long and grown dumb.
Horses rove through them with feeble manes.
Out of breath from the joy of freedom,
these horses didn't know the chase, reins,
bridle and saddle, kicks at ankles.
They trampled underfoot
the burden of blinders and the chains of badges.
They were tired but brisk, feverish lovers of liberty
in a game with wind and stars. Oh yes, the stars—
sad candlesticks, still big in the dingy
candelabra of heaven, amid the wax bodies of planets.

2.

We have never been cavalry horses.
We were horses not identical in color, not running in rank,
not of a noble breed, not well trained, not very courageous,
having no amulet against the evil eye on the road,
losing hooves on streets with paved sidewalks, frothing
furiously at the mouth from the stench of cut down poplar trees.
We were horses sometimes peaceful and silent, sometimes
raging poisons. We could find a ford through mud and
gates leading to the next yard in residential areas.
We stamped our feet, enjoyed our bread and hay—
the soul of the prodigal son—
and went on further to the Martian path
toward the Martians who, we believed,
were rich, long-living and easy-going.
We were horses and ran together
through the scents of mowed grass, awakened embers,
and melting snow flowing down the slope.
We were not cavalry horses.

The Well-Disposed Week

This is the week of happy lingering,
the sensation of going barefoot,
overtones weigh heavily between grapes
and words, are dissolved by the triads.
This is the week of going home;
finally I am where I come from, I have words;
my language and my day have come together.
Not in the plaster casts of actors' feet
exhibited in the foyer, nor in the bars
with their long menus, large plates and small portions,
not in the indifferent glances of passersby
when we laugh out loud.
In those spaces in between,
where the icons on the walls drink from our glasses,
Akhmatova and Brodsky argue about
the responsibilities of the poet,
and words avoid translation.
Words like "Shopping and Fucking"—
legends for others—
a trial even outside the theater, sadly.
Cars raise the alarm when a cat brushes past,
highly sensitive creatures, they quiver when touched.
People submit without making a sound—
at least I've never heard them raise the alarm.
But I'm happy; that hasn't happened in a long time.
The grapes grow heavy,
the sun shifts my cares and responsibilities to the north,

August is coming,
I've forgotten that I have become a cyborg,
have forgotten the direction of my wanderings,
have come home.

There are no refugees anymore
We all can go back

I will be coming
Still I'll be coming

Will steal a glance of the mountain green
covered in the belched grease of steel mills
Will capture in the recorder
voices of some villages and a couple of towns
Will help plant potatoes
and market economy
Will go hungry for some time with my relatives
and take with me homemade tomato paste

And maybe
on streets with new names
will step on my old sidewalks
will thaw some snow as a relish with the brandy
and will pass by

Captured in Light

in the dark i often ask myself whether you feel
the words' shine and see their souls unfurled
around me fall flags and stones and children cry
they'll never learn the taste of milk while
stars pour around you on the islands of my soul
words' shadows play and torture me
the souls of my tongue untranslatable into verse
or into your tribe's tongue to you i come into light
far from myself to be exiled does it mean longing for light
but is light not words my tongue wanders inside me
we're alone my tongue and me and we're captured in light
i wish you could understand how much i miss its freedom
for the darkness of the depths i am drowning and thirsty

II.
Intersection Graph

A Memory about Love

I don't know if I told you that I love you
I don't remember
Too many loose sheets in my day
with important notes
When to meet sponsors
when squanderers
at what time must I be ready with the radio report
how many pages would make the play too long
what type of dialogue does the director prefer
that I should buy tomatoes and zucchini and rice
the report for the consulting company in Basel
we need milk as well
and floor paint
a telephone line with Sofia is essential
and with Arizona and Hamburg
my letters to Tokyo
and to my mother
a birthday card for Ivan
and a thank you card for Ms. Angelou
an appointment to notarize the diploma
a new driver's license
information about the feminist conference in Australia
return the empty bottles to the store
separate paper from the rest of the garbage
there is no detergent for the washing machine
use the computer modem to fax
make an appointment for the tropical vaccination

blood examination
another visit to the dentist
help Jane with the baby
five of my books to the Palo Alto bookstore
call the graphic designer on the way
get the program list of Literaturhaus
use of verbs with indirect objects in the German dative case
set the dishwasher
the American exhibit in Martin-Gropius-Bau
the translation of Derrida
the *New York Times* of yesterday about the Croatian war
our government news from Nikolov at the Bulgarian consulate
read Canetti to the end
get through the Treuhand papers
briefing with partners
on economy related research in Brandenburg
meet John at 5 p.m.
the manuscript for the publishing house in Stuttgart
discuss the London edition with Chantal on Skype
of drama by East European playwrights
watch the discussion on Channel 2
talk with Jenny and Baharov about the recording
take the dog out for a walk
shower, supper, no matter in which order
Little notes
reminders
the plan for the day

I guess I have told you that I love you
if it is not on my important-for-the-day list.

Terminology

to Dolores, for the philosophy of feminism which has little to do with social movements and much more with the right of existence for different points of view

We create a killer cell. It's transferred into the patient. It expands, it seeks its peptide, it kills. The tumor weakens, diminishes, gets smaller piece after piece, and dies. We have won against one of the billions of diseases that eradicate us. A new victory in the war against body invaders. The war of the machines and computers against us. The one that cyborgs have declared on us. Our enemy is not that important whether it be the gods of the seas and hunting, bewitching storms, lions and tigers—it's still war. We create the next killer—a stone, gunpowder, a poison, an electrical shock, a cell. A killer of tumors. This time tumors. In order to live we have killed ourselves with our fiction-making of killers.

I have asked the immunologist how she feels after manufacturing the killer. She is proud, makes a patent, and sells it to a pharmaceutical group. My immune system hopes there will be no need for it to take part in the war between the tumor and its killer. Aren't there non-military notions in life? Aren't there other words in the vocabulary of all languages on Earth, and are all sounds pronounced only through male teeth? On the floor of the lab moves a small spider crab. It's not cancer. I don't want to kill it.

from Underwater Electricity

~

I woke up in your dream—
superfluous words and curtains.
I woke up and threw them
through the open window's summons.
The birds smiled
ambiguously.

If in the morning I cannot comb my hair
because dreams are entwined in it—
you dream of me.

~

Crystal beam in the rapids.
Delight from the movement of the water.
The lines of your angular yet smooth body.
A mountain bleached by the summer.
Splashes of sweat and splashes of laughter on my hair.
A resting sea in the distance.

~

Love—a mussel
calling me from the shore
and from the bottom of the sea.

Three Times »Not«

Not by chance I like to make love on the floor
and write on my knees.
I don't like the unstable surfaces of beds and tables.
A cradle should not pretend to stand firm.

I am an avalanche

I am an avalanche. I fall fondly
snow white
to caress you.

*

Sun in the pebble.
In the tree the amber ripens.
Quantum wind is dwindling.

*

Hope grows in the woman
when she looks through the window,
aware of the shivering sunset.

*

Ice flows in the creek,
of closeness and questions
split light.

*

Ice crystals
braided in the hair,
a touch of farewell.

An Accidental Lesson

I learned from you that I am benevolent,
and that I live properly,
that my way to correct my right decisions
is also correct,
that the merging of all things I believe
has nothing to do
with the universality I am accused of,
and how I distinguish evil
is a part of the evil itself
and simultaneously its demise, that I
can love without feeling guilty
and poles are unnecessary for attraction,
that the loophole in the fence is just
a small passage and not a bridge,
that bridges are an illusion
that every entrance and exit needs
to negotiate with each other
and at the same time offers a choice,
and that if I tie my hair
into a ponytail, I can successfully
scare off mosquitoes,
that my hair is beautiful,
and unbound it's even more so.

Grounded

That's the horror, my girl, my little daughter.
The terrible thought: I will lose you.
I don't even know your name.
Only since yesterday I know that you're a girl.
I foresee your torments and victories—
the daughters still stuck repeating their mothers.
The runway was short
and the plane landed abruptly.
You screamed, I heard your swelling—
my cervix sent the pain out into the world,
forgot the sun, forgot that water has a taste,
pulled itself together in a ball of nerves.
"If you do not bleed, everything is fine,"
said the doctor, one of those calm and balanced people
I always feel unworthy of.
I laid for centuries until I became one with the stones.
The ocean grounded your voice with them,
and what remained was the soft murmuring
of a fetus of the female gender.
And I thought that was only me, though pregnant.

The Bees

Cloning is embedded in the bee.
Could you really distinguish one from the other?
They buzz about your eyes, drink up joy
the nectar of light, and darken the pupils even more.
The bees thicken the honey,
their wax polishes your eyeglasses,
and you see more clearly than before.
Tart poems.
Sugar ceding to bitterness in the coupling.
I remember the corner with a movie theater and flowers,
the beer, the laughter tasting like raspberries.
Flashes of youth and hope.
A flood. Detachment.
But the cloning supposes being,
supposes our children and poems, the honey.
And when we are dying, we prove the same,
unable to bear the pain
after such labor to sting. Life
again and again produces the same bee. And
what a delight—
not only hornet's nests and dayflies
or one-day wonders emerge.

Conversation

guzzled everything save dry water ...
—Joseph Brodsky

She:

Don't turn in your grave. You began
to give existence other names.
Said, I shall call you Bulgaria,
just as Cleopatra was called Egypt.
Stubbed out one cigarette after another
in our hostess' flowerpots,
sweat glistening on your forehead.
Told me once again to read Cavafy,
to think about the road to Ithaka.
And you would have liked to be the woman I was
and remained, strong Penelope who believed in Ithaka,
much more in Ithaka and Odysseus than in the road.
Your aimless wandering, your visions,
life's call exhausted you
because they were merely the road. Let me save you—
I shall call you Odysseus
at least in the picture where in the middle of the rain
your body departed from this world,
from me, into nowhere, rearing up
because Ithaka is necessary for the road.
And then I will open the books,
you and Homer next to each other.

and I will cry; it will smell of tobacco, sweat,
man and ink.

He:

Go to the window, hear how the words fall.
Who is Herbert, who is Auden, and
do we even need to mention Rilke?
In Venice water acquires its poetic meaning:
look how the angels beat out the rhythm—
how dare you write without rhymes?
Caress the sheets of paper, respect demands it.
Has anybody written poetry in the Balkans since Orpheus,
and what is there left for a woman to say after Akhmatova?

She:

You're mean, and you're sexist,
a Russian Jew who left for the West,
you are the God of my youth. Your poems
live on between the autumn leaves.
We wrote them down there, convinced
no one could catch us.
We believed in the decay of matter.
Here and there traces of ink:

your forbidden unrhymed poems.
I didn't remember them.
They altered only my metabolism.
Enough poetry. Give me a sip
of your cup of coffee without sugar.
I know you're guzzling dry water now too …

The Mountains, a Man, a Woman

1.

Who sent him to walk the mountains?
Nobody. And precisely that characterizes the right of man.

He envies the Aboriginals of Australia their
holy ones, which cannot be climbed, nor conquered.
In Europe the mountains shine blue and silver, white and green.
They have surrendered their spirit stories, are seldom red.
Only Etna's embers
remember Odysseus and his crew.

The man ascends slowly,
takes a deep breath in, lets an even deeper breath out.
He has prepared well for this expedition
his whole life long.

The woman is in a hurry, suddenly
she is still young and young again.
She doesn't see the flowers at the edge of the path,
follows the lava flows, she wants to bathe in magma up at the top.
She couldn't care less about the end of life.

A woman never worries about the end, and were she old,
only ever about the beginning.

The man treads carefully, chooses his stones,
scarcely speaks, casts shadows when he looks up at the sun.

His shadow merges with the shadow of the mountain
in the woman's eyes.
She lifts her arms to embrace him.
They turn into flames.

2.

The man is always thirsty
when he has conquered a mountain.
He longs for the water of her breasts
and of her mouth.
She gives him the thermos of tea
to revive him.
She will have him once his thirst has been quenched.

3.

The man loves the mountains again and again.
The woman loves the man. The mountains are a part of her.

What do you love more, the mountains or the sea?
she asks.
Mountains and sea, he replies.

4.

At the top the snow has petrified,
conceals the lava.
A crystal desert alongside boulders born of ash.
The air is thin but the vista
calms the eyes.

The woman plunges into the blue.
A quantum is a unit of light
as a snowflake is a unit of snow.
Is a drop of magma
a reflection of this story,
passes through her head as she falls in flight,
as a drop of ocean
is a reflection of this mountain?
She thinks of the Cyclopes and Troy,
how Achilles decided to become history
and made himself vulnerable for it.
Of Poseidon and
the fact that everybody should accept their lot.
Of Penelope's sea.
Then she herself is in the sea and
the sea water thirsts for her wishes.

5.

Orpheus and his mountains, his songs
are what her body remembers,
childhood.

From the sea the mountains look like
sleeping cats, curled up
into their shoulders and paws,
ready to rise at any moment.

She nuzzles her neck against the smoothness of the water.
The sea is growing cold.

6.

The man
on the mountain
watches.
The woman has survived,
that's good.
She was right to fall,
she likes to dive.

The man wishes the snow were lava.
He's going to descend now,
perhaps he'll make it.

7.

The woman reaches the shore,
freezes in the shadow of the mountain.
Why didn't he jump with her?

8.

The woman forgives his hurry,
she has grown used to him.
The man is preparing for his death
and his life after death.
She'd like him to stay today.

The woman memorizes the smells of his embrace.
Wrapped in the cord of his ligaments
and his longing
she begins to live her story without him.

The shadows of the mountains on the surface of the waves
and in her eyes
remain.

Happiness after Reading
Schopenhauer in California

1.

Along the roses, between their petals, time travels in drops.
Is a petal still alive after it has been plucked?
Children are wonderful at this age when
they no longer bite their nails,
when their features are finely drawn,
framed by their hair and with a smile
that proudly reveals Mona Lisa's likeness.
And time rolls on like loaves of bread and buns,
with no sign yet of mold,
stashed between schoolbooks in a satchel
nibbled by milk teeth and by the other kind,
all arranged in sequential harmony.
Growing up is wonderful,
a kitty cat and a lava horse,
a terracotta warrior from Xian and a teddy bear.
How lovely, how wonderful, the touch
of petals, pointed and smooth, green and pink,
the joy of being ten, being loved, being healthy,
at peace and at school with your friends.
What else can one say about a mother's happiness?
Between the roses of Sofia, Berlin or Los Angeles.

2.

We climb under the splash of the waterfall
through the rainbow, up the mountain,
wet and immediately dried by the sun's rays,
then soaked again and glowing
in the cycle of water and sun.
Later the heat sticks to our thighs,
we are very near the earth's core,
our cells are being sucked dry. Yosemite, Zion, Death Valley,
rain from yesterday or from a thousand years ago.
The difference between the deserts of snow
and salt isn't borne out by their names.
(Is one of them somehow less dead
simply because we don't refer to it that way?)
And each time happiness is measured
in drops of water contained in plastic bottles,
which we bought, then emptied, a moment ago.

3.

The Navajo won't look you in the eye.
Here I recover from the superficial
gaze outside the reservation.
Is the star of which only rays survive
a sun or black hole?
It has been dead for a long time.
It's either nothing or something else,
but its rays reach us and touch our pupils.
Is anybody well enough acquainted with the dead stars
to have earned the happiness of giving birth to them once more?

4.

Because pleasure and enjoyment are not a given,
and you can really only trust pain,
and because imagination doesn't tame the everyday
infecting it with hopes and fears instead,
going to one party on Saturday isn't enough.
Go to a succession of parties, plays,
films, exhibitions, shows, beach volleyball tournaments
and don't miss the school children's concert,
the first graders' rock group, the immigrant kids,
jamming with Jack Nicholson's grandchildren.

5.

Poetry vanished from words long ago,
words were never in poetry.
That much is obvious.
And so is something else—
poetry nests on the façade of the fire station
(or was it the police station?) in American Venice
and traces the tracks made by cheeky pigeons
on Venezia's palace walls.
Who dares maintain that happiness is apposite
and has a fixed location?

6.

On the subject of happiness, *Glück*—ah, that wonderful word!—
I recommend Schopenhauer.
My analysis is subjective, it compares sounds.
Glück has lots of *Lücken,*
luck rhymes with muck and stuck.
In Bulgarian, *щастие,* happiness is often hard to swallow;
there's a lot of *s* and *t*, lots of *sht.*
And *sh*: shallow, shabby, shameful, shambolic, shackled.
Happiness is happenstance.
Schtastie and its various swallowings
are so interesting to explore.
Not the tortuous desire for happiness, but an honest stutter
pops up in the other languages.
Happiness trips up on the *p.*
Glück glugs down the throat.
Kasmet, in fact should be pronounced kismet,
curdles and goes sour when it's kept outside the fridge,
you're unable to swallow it and develop a convulsive stutter
on the *a*, or on the *i.*
The containers where we store our happiness
are not without significance.

III.
Unlost in Translation

Hand Full of Water

We wander through language, we wander,
и не земя, вода на длан ни е нужна,
for we have learned to thirst.
We learned it from the water, the water
That knows no rest by day or night
Always picturing its flight, the water.

Language is like water.
In stasis it slips away,
in flow it finds its form,
feeds more than it drowns,
will not wash away stains,
is the reason shoots emerge.

Тръгнала Румяна за вода студена, леле,
тръгнала Румяна за вода студена.
Живата вода търсила, леле, живата.
The young woman wanted water, water,
cold and lively, water.
A young man came her way, wanted
to drink from her vessels, profess his love.
You do not need a vessel, she said,
to drink water.
Water is like language.

Do not take a ladle, do not take a cup,
do not take a handful.

Drink from the source.
И я остави на мира, водата,
и го остави на мира, езика,
and please let me
use words and grammar
as I see fit.

And
let it take its leave,
the water,
and let language take its leave,
and wander,
and let me
take my
leave

let me take my leave,
take my leave and wander.

Ayran, Boza and Fruit Juices

I'm writing to you, dear colleague,
during a bus ride from Sofia to Plovdiv.
Thus I can't compete with the height
of your thoughts on overseas flights,
but at least I'm traveling
in the direction of Orpheus' mountains—
that has always been my rescue.
And I'm not sending this letter electronically,
which is rare in our circles today
and could be an advantage.

I intend to spend the day in your style:
Ayran, boza and many fruit juices
can be found in Plovdiv just as easily as good wines.
Lately, I almost share your skepticism
toward alcohol and tobacco.
I promise to respond to your questions
about delight
another time. Today I'm
more inclined to dusty Balkan thoughts,
which first of all need water.

The distant mountains look like paper cutouts.
It smells like snow, even though it's still green
all around. Smells are an important indicator, aren't they?
They participate the least in general self-deception.
The form, you say, earns the desire.

But I don't like discussions about form and content.
I'm interested in the processes,
which connect one with the other—
how bodies form and how forms fill up.
We return to that later.

Is there fog over Florence?
What is the Italian word for fog that
cloaks the fields and leaves the mountains free?
When shall we drive to a non-European city,
one of those you mention in your letter?
Meanwhile I've been to so many cities
that I tend not to visit new ones.
Your suggestion, however, makes me curious.
Since nothingness is just the boredom
which replaces curiosity, and we—
didn't we talk about it?—
definitely prefer to live in this world now
rather than stay in eternity.

It's time to warn you
that I often sneeze in oriental places
probably due to the spices in the air.
One cannot predict if you like this—
although there are advantages since
you can't lose me in a crowd—
but I guess your hearing will be greatly disturbed.

Oh yes, I would be very happy to cooperate
should the project on the globalization
of knowledge get a chance.
Otherwise we could continue to try exchanging unsharable
experiences. What a thrilling challenge!
Maybe you already notice how my letters
are tightrope dancing in this bus?
I hope they manage to reach your end.

I wonder what you're doing now.
Please, tell me about it retrospectively—
look at your calendar:
October 15th, 8 a.m.
Still sleeping? Making love? On the way to work? Reading?
Brushing teeth? A meeting in the tea room?
Simultaneity interests me—
my first idea of time comes from theoretical physics.

But let me leave you alone
and allow myself to look out the window.
After all, I'm in a bus,
not far from the Rhodope Mountains.
See you soon in social media.
Take care of yourself.
Sincerely yours
ts

Ruschuk, Rousse, by the Danube

Back to the future
of my previous past.
I was nine when, at a junction
in this city, a friendly traffic policeman
said "Cut your path straight!"
when I asked him how to
reach the delta of the river, which back then
could be reached neither one way nor the other.
On the opposite bank: the factory,
another one of our pasts, a
Romanian one, the pride of Ceaucescu.
It meant no present in which
that blue, yellow, gray, wonderful
air over the Danube could be clear—
that's how Ecoglasnost began, my '89.

An excursion to the future
of bygone future plans.
What awaits me there? Which
Land Rovers and Mc's, which Donald at the wheel,
which tongues that have already devoured
our tongues—mine and Canetti's—
braised in a pot of clay and heavily seasoned
to facilitate forgetting? Forgetting
that you could reach them today, the delta
and the source. But in Rousse people
who know the way are always turning up,

and they are often verbose angels, and I
heed their words, cut my path straight,
and sew myself a coat of maps.
It allows me to fly, and from above—
this time the air is more transparent—
delta and source coalesce. There is
only the river, no past, no time.
From Gertrude Stein's perspective
clarity reigns over the water,
which neither separates nor connects,
only flows. And I land, bewitched, by the sea,
which takes off my paper coat and loves me.
That's how simple things can be
if you don't insist on their being otherwise.

Forwarded Greetings

This stubborn horse
I will beat for an hour,
and if needed two hours long,
until it reveals the right words.
—Konstantin Pavlov, *Alchemist*

Levchev the elder
once told Sonja and she told me
the story about a horse from Sofia
(and I thought only Konstantin Pavlov
knows something about horses).
In a park near his apartment,
there was a shack, a cultural monument made of wood,
that even he, a writers' union chairman in communist times,
could not save, so it was destroyed.
Once upon a time there was a poet—
Vutimski—who back in 1983 blew our minds
with his astonishing verse that so disturbed
the government no textbook could include it.
A classmate with a joint in his mouth read to me
this poetry from pages copied by hand.

Vutimski was poor, homeless and unemployed.
One day he was hired as a park keeper, yet
because there was no such civic job description,
he was added to the city's budget
in the category "horses"—

this many coins for horseshoes,
this amount for hay and apples, a little more
for carrots, riding and coat brushing.
And so he survived in the wooden shack in the park.

Was Vutimski translated into English?
The poet-horse. Here a poet can be anything.
He can even chat with God and not to us anymore.
With her hands, Sonja described how
Konstantin stopped speaking out after the stroke
because fortune took his tongue.
His gestures were clear and needed no interpretation.

"He died," I wrote yesterday in an e-mail in several languages,
as if language knows something about death.
"In your cities, pour a drop of wine from your glasses
on the earth, as in the old Bulgarian custom,"
I wrote. "The earth will know what to do next."
"Don't be sad," an answer came at night.
"Konstantin will send greetings to all poets and horses,
from us who don't yet know
if we choose horse or poet."

The Gardener

The gardener builds a new wall
from old stones. Old stones, he calls
proudly, nothing gets lost in this world.
—Michael Krüger

He didn't know that black holes were stars
and wasn't interested in outer space.
We sat, drank nothing, he had to
turn over too many leafs.
I sensed he had become someone else—
ein anderer rather than *дрyг*—
not the Russian word for friend,
but the German for different.

He did his best in the garden. The flood
turned out to be caused by a single tear
for which the mountains came down to the water
and the seas whitened, longing for higher peaks.

Right now the wind is thoroughly cleaning
the gardener's hands.

Courting Europe

We met nowhere
but we always wanted to have breakfast,
smell the early morning coffee, get acquainted.
"Good morning!" Europe splutters.
A little extra foam. Seduction at the rim.
A creamy tornado builds in a cup,
a lone black stripe at the center.
(Espresso, express, French press?)
We age faster than we think.
Pleasure. A temptation of union,
an advance on wished for dreams.
We can conceive of orgasms,
even experience some that never took place—
those where peoples
pass constitutions in a collective frenzy.
And you charm me into inhabiting new places.
(Only yesterday I was ready to give up on life.)
Mischievous cells dance on my lips,
multiply exponentially.
Choose life, you say, quickly
commit to slowness.
And court the expansion of the future.

The Beginning and the End of the Metaphor

Дий, водно конче!
Вдишай
доверие в деня.

Giddy-up, dragonfly!
Breathe
confidence from the day.

Giddy-up, my horse!
I can take you to the water to drink myself.

Giddy-up, water horse!
Breathe! All my words
I take straight from the horse's mouth.

Giddy-up, hippocampus!
Breathe, brain!

Hüh, Seepferdchen!
Atme
Vertrauen in den Tag.

Giddy-up, sea horse!
Breathe
confidence into the day.

The Speech of the Female Translator

I wove only words with their many meanings,
looking for the light they share,
I dug out the hidden parts of the dodo from the ashes,
took the ones I found out of the glass case,
threw the dictionary of deception into the river.

(A lot of time went by loving the letters,
I had to draw them tenderly all over again,
and erase when needed to make them reborn.)
Often I crossed without using the bridges I'd built.

On the other banks I smiled absently—
I found the sources I'd always believed in,
filled the jars, drank until my thirst was satisfied,
refilled them, dreaming of pure water

(and gave away everything to a book).

Poetry and Philosophy of the Presence

three seconds and again three seconds
hold breath, snore in German
my husband could perhaps snore in Bulgarian
like my brother, this is
a scary incest dream
so I get up, pace the floor back
and forth and count
three seconds and a break
again that much and once more a pause
constant repetition
I am a Mickey Mouse
a Celtic god with big ears who can
only hear

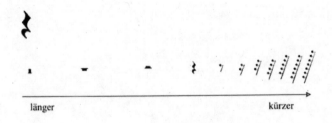

Bathrobe

Where is my bathrobe?
On the dryer.
Which dryer?
The tumble dryer next to the washer.
Where is the washer?
In the bathroom.
But where is the bathroom?
In the house! Or did you take a shower outside?
And the house, where is that?
In the garden, you joker.
And where is the garden?
In the village, it's in the village!
But where is the village?
In western Bulgaria.
And where is that?
Learn geography! Obviously in the Balkans.
In what?
A peninsula in southern Europe.
You? Rope?
The continent, of course!
What is that?
The land between oceans and seas, Eurasia.
Where can I find that?
On the planet!
But which planet?
Earth, in our solar system.
This system of sun and stuff, where is that?

In the middle of the Milky Way.
The Milky Way?
It's part of our galaxy.
And that is?
Our part of the universe.
U-ner-vous?
Yes.
But, Mom, where is this u-nerve-verse?
In the hands of God, my dear.
And God, Mama, where can I find him?
Well, go search for him yourself—
do I need to tell you everything?

Mom, Mom, look! He's in the pocket of my bathrobe!
There you go! Be careful when you hang it.

Violet's Wayfairing Tales

… a small girl climbing a mountain. A courageous, confident girl
carves her name in a tree trunk … all the way around …
(after Gertrude Stein)

> The paths of seed and stipe, of gardener and visitor cross
> there, the way they do in the dust, in the sand and pebbles,
> in fertilizer and foliage, in the earth and in the air.
> Walking is a garden method of getting from A to B.

Growing up in the Balkans means frequent changes of name. I
grew up, variously, as Теменужка, Теменуга, Йонка, Μενεζές,
Βιολέτα, Menekşe, Sigliah, Фиалка, Љубичица, Ljubicasta and
Vijolica.

> Stopping to rest is part of it, as is starting over.

Flowers of love cover the wedding bed of Hera and Zeus. Violet
secrets were concealed in the Oriental *harbinger of love*, Slavic *тъма
и нега*, darkness and longing, were woven together in one word.

> Sowing and planting. Bringing happiness, and feeling it.

Even within a family, names change frequently to protect a child
from the evil eye. I was Nuscha, Tami, Meni, Tete, Jonka, Rushka.
How can you take identity seriously in the Balkans?

Make tea and wait for sunset: time as layers of happy
moments. An aromatic soup brings joy for a whole day,
a person lasts for several weeks. But, as the proverb says,
there is only one way for a person to be happy a whole life
long: by planting a garden.

At the international holiday camp by the sea, the name Temenuzhschka,
with its many consonants so close together, can only be pronounced
incorrectly. Within a few hours I am given several more names:
Violet, Fiolka, Jolanda, Olopu, Orvokki, Pamakani, Nauda,
Našlaitė, Violetiné, Yalanthe, Violetta, Sumire, Viooltje, Fialki,
Tyrsfolia, Viona, Jonka … I become a garden, cultivating many
languages.

Hydrangea and carnations are bearers of happiness in the
Balkans; tulips bring joy, as do rosebushes; behind them dwell
rabbits and centaurs. Journeys of discovery with Alice and
Athena bear scratched elbows in their wake.

Friendships through letters, always written twice: once in one's own
language and then again in a common language. Being a garden
was the only way to survive the era of real socialism. Which was
the name given to the everyday back then.

A child prefers to find its own paths, off the beaten track.
The child breathes in peonies and rosebuds, calendula and
snapdragon, violets and lilacs, linden, cherry, walnut and
quince trees. A child has a lot of time to study scents.

I always found kindred spirits: There are 207 species of my kind in Latin alone. Acuminata, adunca, appalachiensis, blanda, calaminaria, lanceolata, lobata, obtusa, praemorsa, purpurea, riviniana, subsinuata, tripartita, wittrockiana, suavis, riviniana, odorata … The Balkan violet *viola gracilis* signifies grace, Hawaii has its *viola chamissioniana robusta*. Hawaii and the Balkans, by the way, are exactly opposite each other on the globe. You are not only yourself, but also your own opposite I.

> It is worth planting gardens with memories of flowers that smell like language. Sdravetz, the rock cranesbill geranium, which honors the holy inventors of the Slavic alphabet, lends itself particularly well to this: It is easy to care for, resistant and adaptable all at the same time.

Thus, when it came to identity, I always had one foot in botany and the other in astrophysics. Whenever I tried to arrive at a historical definition, I always came back to the different names of plants. Whenever I wanted to arrive at a geographical definition, I couldn't summon up any maps, but pictured the earth as a celestial body.

> A ficus leaf from the courtyard of a Californian university could cross the ocean without coming to any harm at the end of the eighties. That's not possible anymore. From its pot in Berlin it stretches up toward the light. Greenhouses are obviously important when it comes to replanting.

I am of medium height and need direct sunlight for a minimum of several hours a day. I can be left in the garden all year round, can spend an endless amount of time in gardens.

When the gardener is away, the flowers are in danger. But normally they wait, are trusting, ration their water and food, and revive upon your return.

At the *Veigerlfest* I am celebrated as a lovely harbinger of spring. The language of this festival makes me rejoice in its tones.

Chamisso's garden is always full of shadows; that's why the sun is more enjoyable there than in other gardens. And I believe him: "Blow on the frost and it will disappear."

The bird's voices are loud this year in the grand competition for love and territory. It was a long winter and now they are busy making up for it. The colors of the buds compete with bird song for attention. I used to think that the senses complement each other, but now I'm no longer sure.

To discover and identify seeds and scions or bulbs I like to go to abandoned gardens. Today's gardeners are hectic and too numerous.

I became aware that a flower is a place, that I myself am a place, when Dauthendey confessed that after his four-month journey through Asia, in Japan he finally felt as though he had arrived in his Franconian home because of the violets blossoming on the edge of the path.

As he walked around Weimar, Goethe, the gardener, always had violet seeds in his coat pocket so that he could strew them in appropriate places. What was his understanding of appropriate?

For the physicist and poet Goethe, and for later figures of his ilk, happiness consisted of the harmonious co-existence of many, often irreconcilable things.

As a gardener you learn stamina and to only ever do the next thing that lies before you. Layer by layer "Geh, Hirn," "Hüh, Seepferdchen! Atme" and other sediments are deposited.

I don't have to decide between colors and song; the question is rather how my airways will get along with all these trees and flowers blooming at the same time. I sneeze, cough, cry, rub my eyes—all this in celebration of them, an appreciative sacrifice.

Breathing and walking at the same time: the highest level of happiness.

There are less and less uncultivated mushrooms in our gardens, beginnings are becoming more and more difficult, and the greatest happiness of all—being a beginner—is becoming more and more rare. Rilke smiles behind the flowerbed containing the moon-sized peonies.

Seeing: The dark earth has a brighter effect on us than the stars. It's thanks to both of them that we grow.

Celan, more than anybody else, knows about walking. It was he who led me to admire the seedhead of a dandelion before it became a dandelion plant.

I will walk through the garden and launch dandelion balloons.

I would have preferred to remain nameless, but that's not easy for a flower with too many names, and names that are always changing.

Before I send the dandelion flying in all directions, I write on it:

Temenuzhschka is a viola is a violet is a menexes is a ljubicasta is an orvokki is a fialka, is an olopu is a nuscha, is a pamakani, is a sigliah is a vijolica is one and many, is one and the same all the way around the globe.

Im Schwarzwald — чернозем.

IV.
Trajectories and Latitudes

Taking Flight

Hear anew the voice! O hear and listen!
—Sappho

Daedalos or Dedalus, Daidalo *Дедал Деда* loss.
Deadalo (n.): deadly fall and deadline for taking off.
Take a flight with or takeoff without Dad.

We all know he is the best and can do everything.
He collects the flight lore, knows about arrival—
his own without the child, without the woman
who is even more unreasonable
and ties herself to a tree like fastening wings.

And she speaks: "I wish to atone
for the birds of migration,
careless words—
feathers scattered in rapid passing,
unintended mistakes—
nests abandoned in the search, left to grow cold.
I long to understand
my closeness to the sun—
my guide and fellow traveler
and an obsession that enchants me:
Come then
now, dear goddess, and release me
From my anguish. All my heart's desiring
Grant thou now. Now too again as aforetime,
Be thou my ally.

Only emptiness separates me from the Earth,
the distance of a bird's glance.
I fly inside clouds of down and on my arms
quills break out of shivering skin. I fledge.
I lose my sense of touch, my taste for lovesickness.
My eyes sharpen. Oh Earth!
In my flight across latitudes
in the dizziness of endeavoring,
the Earth is in my all-embracing view,
and the tree pays with its roots,
with the green of my eyes,
with the beak of the woodpecker for whom
the forest is more important than freedom.
I, Sappho, renounce love.
I become a clenched compact missile
and cleave the air.
My skin—the smooth one that loved the hands
of the wind, blades of grass and lovers' arms,
my skin elongated into bird's sin
before I fall into the sea."

Oh, white cliffs of Lefkada, far from Crete.
What else do we inherit but choice,
not to go near the water or to plunge into surf.
Icarus competed with Sappho, not with his father.
He wanted to craft wings from verses.

Daedalos wished he could understand his son,
avoided winds of all kinds,
as if flying without wind were possible to master.

She accelerates—тя се спуска спуска се спусъкът целта,
flying up, down, ahead, straight, forward, farther.
One, two, three: Look sharp! Go! *Los!*
Caresse sur l'océan, oh, et l'oiseaux …
Whether the ocean wants her, she doesn't know.
Her lovers didn't want her.
The casual acquaintances didn't as well.
Her daughters didn't want to be with her either.
Calme sur l'océan. Will she turn into a whale
like Daedalos? He who used to be a land creature,
a huge dog, a big shot, a beast, in love
with the goddess of curiosity.
He, who learned swimming in midair.
No, she is no whale and no bird, she simply loves.
There ain't not much future for a man who works the sea
but there ain't no island left for islanders like me.

Here she is—Sappho flying. Alone. No Icarus.
No Daedalo, who mastered the art of navigating
in the air, who adored cybernetics,
who compiled the operation manual of our world,
and wired in the beginning our social media posts.
Today nobody knows exactly who's who

and whether SMS or SOS is needed.
Nobody knows about Sappho's flight and Daidalos' death,
about Daedalus as a hybrid creature, a whale,
who breathes in one language and swims in another,
remembers in one and dreams in another,
departs in the first and arrives in the other.

She—a dead bird's body that flies.
She—sun of Lesbos and sun of Andros,
wife of a man from the Cyclades
to whom she bore a daughter,
Kerkylas from the isle of Andros,
the κέρκος of Heracles.
She—не е кукла, пише стихове, има дъщери,
exiled to Etna,
but everywhere the snow can turn into hail,
always thin air, only the vastness touches the eyes.
And she leaps into the blue.
At least that's what we know from the storytellers.
They tell a lot, but only these are certain:
"before," "after," "despite," "because,"
"instead of," "for," "nor," "yet" and other such
prepositions and connective words
between her and all those onlookers on Lefkada,
where, bound to a tree or bird, she had to choose
between the white of the cliffs and the white of the surf.
The white belongs to her

though she remembers Daedalus' debts
that were never repaid.
Her skin distinguishes between Sappho and SAPHO
syndromes. Rheumatism mustn't defeat verse.
She isn't ill because she's fledging.
Her daughter, Cleïs, whose hair was torchlight
akin to the lucid language of Kleist,
is still flying. But Sappho doesn't trust anymore.
She only believes in the ocean and the steam,
foam, cloud, spring and river,
ubiquitous water that flows like words flow:
Swift to the darksome earth their course directing,
Waving their thick wings from the highest heaven
Down through the ether.

Let's follow her: - u - x - | u u - u - x
therefore хайде! Now let's sing:
Es blühen in allen Häfen Rosen! tralalalala
Das ist die Liebe der Matrosen, tralalalala
und πάρα δ' έρχετ ώρα (pára d' érchet óra)
vorbei geht die Zeit.
It's too late. Time goes by.
This too will pass.
Ποικιλόθρον multicolored, diverse.
And let us make it as she demands: see above.
A sailor's love is strong but doesn't last long
For that's the way with ev'ry sailor …

107

From admiral to simple whaler…
A wife in ev'ry port—is his idea of sport.
That makes his life a gay one because he knows it's short,
because he knows it's short.
And so when he appears, you can be sure, my dears,
he'll show you paradise but you're bound to end in tears
and πάρα δ' ἔρχετ ὥρα (pára d' érchet óra)
vorbei geht die Zeit. Because it's too late.
Time goes by, and this too will pass.

Why now I called thee;
What for my maddend heart I most was longing?

No, I don't trust the ocean. I tether myself.
On my daughter's birthday we paraglide
in tandem, tied with a belt, prepared
for any coincidence and the illusion of flying.
Crete is still far. Only the lines of Cyprus are in sight,
fluid boundaries between sea and coast
and borders drawn between people.
It's even farther up to Cape Lefkada.
White cliffs full of lies.

Feta means a piece, as in a bite of
red watermelon, a blood corpuscle.
Feta means nothing white; it's only sliced matter.
What has gotten into me? What on Earth

am I talking about? I should fly. Like my daughter.
She borrows more arms from the Indian deities.
All her arms spread wide, ready for flight. And she takes off.
I copy her, tied up in knots.
Am I scared for her or only for myself?

God-Stier, Stoff-Tier, Mensch-Tier, Stier aus Papier,
a bull, fabric-animal, human-bull, bull of paper,
Zeus, Taurus. Minotaur, song, papyrus, screen
Зевс, Таурос, песен, папирус, хартия
екранът обира сега обичта ни
god bull as a paper cut, a bull's eye in the labyrinth,
a screen which robs our ambition and greed.
Daedalus? In the end he won. It's done.
But the sea belongs to us.

Tell us, Dedalus, do you kiss your mother before you go to bed?
Daedalus was heartbroken. *The other fellows
stopped their game and turned round, laughing.*
Now other people commit murders and take flights.
They all laugh again. My body, *hot and confused in a moment.*
What was the right answer to the question?

And I learn the sea.
I'm not a dad who only believed
in flying and teaching his child how to fly.
I am the daughter of my daughter and of Sappho's daughters.

I fly over the sea on the day I give birth.
What I have written here is only myself,
my name and where I was. Class of Elements, the Universe.
What was after the universe? Nothing.
But was there anything round the universe
to show where it stopped before the nothing place began?
Daedalus was heartbroken. I simply give birth.
It was very big to think about everything and everywhere.

Daedalus is long dead. To fly is still to learn.
And it's my turn.

Learn! Учи, учи, то сляпото окато прави!
There's none so blind as those who will not see.
"I will never leave you alone"
I say.
"I'm your mother—
Minotaur and Theseus in one—
even after my death I will not leave you alone."
She jumps.
I jump.
She sings, "Oh, white cliffs!"
I am silent.
Finally
jumping and falling will turn into flight.
And she lives
without me,

flies
without me,
near the sun and the ocean,
near the earth and the star—nothing
is dangerous,
she has taken flight.
Away! Away! The spell of arms and voices:
the white arms of roads, their promise
of close embraces …
April 26. … So be it. Welcome, O life!
I go to encounter for the millionth time
the reality of experience …
April 27. Old father, old artificer, stand me now
and ever in good stead.

So I confess:
I repeatedly equate
Ariadne with the Labyrinth,
Daedalus with Joyce,
Gefangen im Licht = Spiel vom Lichtfangen,
Captured in light = Playing tag with light.
Let me bring to your attention this excuse:
"We have the option somewhere
where we don't need options.
There is no choice in a space
called *Between.*"

I mix up the genes of languages,
denke nicht ob ich Sohn oder Tochter gebäre,
give birth equally to a daughter or a son
who colors the cliffs
white as if canvas.
My daughter flies off radiant
and is even happier when we arrive,
then paraglides again
alone this time
and with no illusions. Δαιδάλλω.

The seas be ours
And by the powers
Where we will, we'll roam
Yo-ho, all together
Hoist the colors high
Heave-ho, thieves and beggars
Never shall we die
likewise Minotaur und Theseus in one.
Dante is the governess of Dad-loss.
The song has been sung. The time is upon us.

Time is running out for us. It is November 9.
I'm in the middle of a nightmare of rebirth.
Ποικιλόφρον and Ποικιλόθρον. It's hard
to decide between these two readings when
they're both meant. I don't get off the chair.

I'm tied to the tablet with a multicolored mind.
My ass doesn't move. My eyes don't close for sleep.
I get fat. I get old. I merge with the cliffs.
I become a wave. I am Sappho, Ari Leshnikoff,
Homer and Dante, the children in The Chorus,
Pirates of the Caribbean, Billy Joel and
James Joyce, a Bulgarian proverb
and a German folksong. I burn
full of traditions, tired in translation
and implantation.
I get burned but not burned out:
I rewrite. I learn the difference between
taking flight and taking off. On my own.

Daidal ja und immer wieder да ида allein
Yes, I come by myself
I come for certain
without her, without him
ohne sie und ohne ihn.
Alone, I said, Dadloss
allein, sagte ich, komme ich:
No Deadalo is needed here.

The Return of the White Bull

In the sea by Ithaka, in the cool of the waves
where the clear water reveals every secret,
crusty rocks folded over like puff pastry,
a library of epics,
I eat them with my eyes.

There he is, white, snorting anger,
the horned beast is on the move again.
The gracious woman exits the myth
to escape him.
He charges onwards, leaps over the mountains,
wants to take her as he did once before
with all the confidence of a god.
She gave herself to him then,
today she wants somebody else.
Apollo's eyes are green.
The bull continues his charge
and when he reaches the sea
he drinks, tears the ground apart.

The sails on our boat flutter,
in the canal between Meganisi and Lefkas
there is little wind, the day is hot and dry.
We sail to the island yearned after
for so many years by Odysseus
for so many years by others after him
and for even more by me.

The captain wants to bring us to other shores,
the gods are not with us, he says,
the winds are unfavorable, will you please
stop talking about Ithaka.
I stare into the haze of the sea,
I long incessantly
for those shores.

The Ionian Sea recognizes me,
and I have journeyed all of Odysseus' routes
and did not arouse Poseidon's anger—
how would I?—
nobody is waiting for me in Ithaka,
it is time for me to reach its shore.
The captain is drinking *Mythos* beer,
opens up the charts,
the lines on his face draw themselves into his tan,
I promise a poem, he comes around.
And as the decision is made, the wind changes,
rocks the boat even more wildly,
and we, our feet anchored to the deck,
can scarcely hold the rudder.

We arrive, and three times on each of three days we try
to drop anchor next to olive trees' thick trunks.
And in three bays Ithaka gives us a friendly smile
and pushes us away,
the anchor slides in seaweed and refuses to grip.

Let's go for a swim at least.
The captain shouts:
"You first,
kiss the holy water."
And his joke will lead to three more angry days
in the three bays,
and a further three times three.

Latitudes

A.

Tall, slim and silent, the firs grow
along the railway line to the southwest.
"Look how much I wrate," the child
struts in the bus. "When I'm done,
I'll draw a bird!" "*Wrote,*" I correct.
"Rate-mate, mate-rate," sings my mind.
There are few old tales about fir forests.
How does the child learn words
that have been blown in the wind?
I don't know what appears to her
when they are gone, firs in the precious
just before, now only fields. The birds
enjoy the wide vista of the bus lane
risking death, they give the child
the chance to observe them.
"Look, I wrate **BIRD**. There, look!"
"Wrote," I repeat. "You wrote."

B.

Conegliano really does exist,
even if the MyPhone
unsmart and un-phonetically
corrects to "congenial."
It's a Prosecco village near Venezia.
"Venezuela, Venice Beach,"
cheekily suggests the MyPhone,
a replica of the Playing Man.
"N? I? C? E? I wrote NICE many times,
many N and lots of ICE. Look, nice!
Do I have holes in my ears? What
do you think? Yeah? All people?
Loopholes in the ears ...
and the words do *not* stay?"

C.

A bus competes with the train
heading toward the mountains.
A hill, long fallen asleep,
dreams of waking up at dusk.
A child draws rhinos and rhymes:
"A rhino wants to eat a lot of fruit;
it really doesn't want to boot.
It hurries there with just three toes,
hits nosy rattle beetle on the nose."
And I trust playing is eternal.

D.

The girl's hair braided with blue flowers
caresses the flying body, calms its eyes.
Gold and wheat color the air.
It becomes easier to trust the sun.
The bird with the blue eyes
is woven into the seat cover,
its feathers are smooth,
matted from frequent pressure.
The girl with the flowers in her hair
gently strokes the surface
as if the threads could unravel
and set the bird free.

Selected Affordable Studio Apartments

Homage for Yvan Goll

I.

Descend the floorless staircase of the centuries

where does the staircase rise, birdlike
each step gives birth to a sun
only a light wind
tethers it to the earth

where is confidence
an airy white dress
passing by
a façade that surrenders
dark windows for sale

how will the boy keep going
my shadow looks at him
he needs three wheels as I three languages
and a companion, or more than one
his feet, his own step
determined

where is the airship flying
that severed its ropes, and mine
I don't know

which was a coincidence and what
I decided for myself

II.

A night, on a road paved with shadows

where does this road lead
while the stones rearrange themselves flat
to prove the earth's curvature
when the lines mirror
the paths of the current
the electricity between ocean and earth
and inform the sky
when cars turn into ships
when skyscrapers become a movie set

how far away from war
does this road lead
full of high voltage
in this desolate world

III.

If we followed the path of the silent trees
and the dumb stones

where are the stones heading
between craggy houses
on rutted paths

where do they come from
how many earths have they left behind
to rise up here

where do they lead
those that have gathered
under steep vaults
past closed doors
in order to propel

the hard work of green summer
upwards
it seems so easy here
to hang Orpheus
on every branch and leaf

light of my clearing
are you up there

IV.

A hundred or a thousand years ago
My footprint was worn in the sand

nourishing, billowing past
still foolish, shortly after carnival
precious future, the arguments ever more unconvincing
flowing entanglements
born yesterday, moving on tomorrow
call me, call today
so that I don't think in a direction
where you are not

V.

Leaning over your eyes
I see backward into the nascence of worlds

joyful women wear bright tights nowadays
and escape flooding in high heels
they prefer tight blouses
and renounce the halo of innocence
they drive to the office everyday
look friendly or glum
color their hair unassertively, post-emancipatedly
don't sleep as often with their bosses
and only occasionally with their beloved
shop before each cinema visit
cook once a week on Sundays to feign interest
their calculations do not include god
and me? a human life long
I see his eyes and yours
opening and closing
closing and opening

VI.

Rien ne va plus

a glass of water nurses flowers
chairs stare at us, and far off
a table could accommodate food
or traces of poems
but there is nothing, absolutely nothing
but emptiness that is an observer
measuring the temperature between inside and out
setting the snapdragons on the roses
air streams in and inflates the lampshade
fraying without fear a sense of home
dreamweed the smile of an absent angel
there is too much emptiness to feel comfortable
gingerly the mountain loses its grip
and silence shakes the sky

VII.

But the sun is not a skull
It is the blossom of the dandelion

the unfathomable rubble below the balcony
a welcoming labyrinth for mice
a safe place to hide from cats and foxes
new buildings are as brave as geranium roots
tirelessly we look after residents and blossoms
solve inequalities, learn how to leap
from the local tree squirrel
explore our stock of guilt and thyme
the sun shines each day for free
and the taxman does not suspect
how many rays of gold we have failed to declare

VIII.

The Saga of our hidden hearts

all those places are gentrified today
selected affordable studio apartments
long-term rental Paris Auteuil, Brooklyn et al.
Rue Raffet rented on YouTube
Villa Emo in Padua everyone's holiday home
interiors, façades, nearby shops
garages, hotels, mountains and squares
forgotten mirrors
photos in the archives
celebrate the peace doves
their flight between places and alphabets

you, Tristan Torsi, Isaac Lang, Jean de Saint-Dié
Ivan Lassang, Johannes Thor, Jean Langeville
Appolinaire's son, Celan's father, Geo Milev's buddy
lightbringer Orpheus, weary Odysseus, Yvan sans Terre
talk to the doves, sitting on dull clouds
that drink in the landscapes of civilization
you take the sun seriously
Every season is good for the heart's labor
any time is good for celebrating those who build

IX.

The one without land is not without a secret

I look for you
in Saratoga Springs Berlin Paris
Rappschwihr Freiburg Birth
Saint Dié Sankt Sveti Manhattan
Padova Brooklyn Lausanne Didel
Rue Raffet Palais d'Orsay
Neuilly-sur-Seine Death
everything means less
I look for you
between oxygen
nitrogen and steam
at home in two places, in love with two people
or everything triple
or not at all
wrapped *in the cloth of the infinite*
in words

X.

In what tongue shall I sing for you now

I must celebrate the words, not only you
for everything that celebrates birth must be named
in order to exist
you are a puma because I call you so
I call you and you are
one of those strong graceful mountain cats
that remain true, hunt only when necessary
walk supple, majestic
and look straight into the eyes
after the Californian
I take the German words
I call your arms arms
and your home my home
in my mother tongue I lack words
since in Bulgarian you firmly promised
to be, and everything
that already exists, resists naming
I want to celebrate you without words

Chestit Rozhden Den!

XI.

And how many lives are needed to become human

this man
who hasn't noticed the woman at the door
who is looking for the woman in the sky
as if she were a pigeon
an airship, a cloud
a more-than-a-woman
this man
who leans out of the window
without routes, ageless
who would like to jump
would like to fly
who wants to become longing
this man
who didn't know
and wasn't afraid to say
that he doesn't know
who we are
what is destiny
chance
naming
the stamp of our desires
what we are who he is who they we
who I

XII.

And with the mill of universe grinding the time

flowers alternate with light
magic circles of non-understanding
here I live, now and then, becoming human
Turning with the wheel which turns in my heart

Twelve

A hand in mother's hand.
She squeezes it.
"You feel cold," she says,
warming my hand
with a worried smile.

On stage The Knight of the Rose—
my Christmas present for her.
Two places in the opera instead of Christmas roses.
My hand searches for hers again.
We are sitting in row 12.
There's light in front of us.
She looks at me astonished: "You feel warm."

The clock's hands are too many—
three overstrain,
to him one is enough.
It should measure the hours,
and if possible stop at night.
It's very confusing
that there shall be twice as many hours
and only twelve ciphers.

Standing in the midday sun I
fear the raspberries will snitch on me
and tell my mother
how many words I have forgotten.
I fear my father's lungs
no longer know how to breathe.

She refuses to eat
or to drink—
she wants to go with him.
She embodies stubbornness, will and
self-determination. She's
furious with God, and with life
and would never allow the Universe
to determine the fate of the Earth.

Wanted is a childhood hero.
There will soon be elections.
I toss and turn the 12 candidates over in my sleep.
Robinson Crusoe got lost in being alone.
The four Musketeers forgot themselves in a battle.
Only Gulliver, oh Gulliver is always himself—
around him Lilliputians, giants, horses
and wonders again, when he becomes real
reading poems in Berlin
in the spirit of Vadim, the storyteller.
The Little Prince remains a hero for grownups.
Jan Bibijan is widely unknown in the West.
Alice from Wonderland is complex and self-sufficient.
You can only envy Pippi Longstocking.
Peter Pan didn't visit our climes for long.
Nothing suits Russian Gulliver far and wide.
Vadim resigns. The elections are in danger.
But you shouldn't forget about Karlsson.
In the ballot for the suitable childhood hero
I vote for Karlsson-on-the-Roof.
I vote for his propellers,
for the motor of the propeller,
for the impulse, the impetus, the wish
to visit a child by flying
without robbing or seducing,
without scaring or overwhelming,
without trying to save,
a visit, just to be there and tell stories.

I took in all the air.
Now everybody breathed me
in-out, in-out, in-out.
All my salts and acids,
cell by cell.
There wasn't much left from me.
I turned into air.
Everyone looked through me.
I suffocated in the blink of an eye,
without air, without myself,
always inhaled and exhaled—
foreign lungs, foreign mouths,
nostrils and trachea,
bloodstreams, brains, and hearts.

"This is the one who scolds.
Look, the evil is coming
from the outside to the inside."
I cross the living room
between the door of the corridor
and the terrace door.
I carry the little rug
woven by his mother
to beat out the dust.
"My mother," he says
about my mother, his wife,
and he is amazed
that I am not her.
I speak in ever louder tones.
For twelve years I cross the border between
the two worlds in the brain of my father.
Between his smart living cells full of love
and those full of dead water.
Hours spent talking about the coup in Istanbul
with concern, about our Foreign Minister,
who is the next German president,
about our newly-elected president in Sofia,
and the poor boat people,
how beautiful the cities
of Aleppo and Benghazi were.
"Inshallah," he says
if someone addresses him in German,

like his Arab colleagues called back then
when the cyclone broke the truck windows
on the border between Chad and Libya.
We talk, drink tea, and he often laughs
at my unfinished sentences, reassures me that
he has lived well despite the hard times,
that he leaves hoping
we have learned something from those
who have made their way to the afterlife.
He says, "The granddaughter's boy,"
meaning her boyfriend,
"is a good fellow. They'll be fine,
don't worry,
here there will be no more wars."
"How do you know that?" I ask,
"They know each other only recently
and war rages very close to us."
He smiles:
"My heart is sick and knows a lot."

Suddenly he remembers
that I'm the bad one
who beats the carpets,
who brings in the cold from the outside.
I should be his wife or his mother
because I care for him. But I am neither.
So we sway in the cradle of old age every day.
He is only confused
if something hurts him a lot,
when his blood sugar shoots up,
if forced to be someone
other than himself,
when his freedom-loving soul is caged,
if he did not drink enough water
and, and, and …
Apart from that
his cells are full with life,
maybe overfilled. Disciplined they take
the unhealthy ones along. Tenaciously they both
manage to get up,
to stand upright,
go to the toilet or
distinguish words and sounds.
Together all his cells
meet the light every day
and exorcize demons.

I believe they will recognize
the moment when his light
is closer to God than to us.
It beams out of the birch bark,
out of the clouds
that have collected sunlight in their drops,
out of the kitten fur
and the green of my eyes.
How long will the blue
glow in my father's?
"Wait for me,"
I tell him and go to work,
"Don't go away,
while I'm not yet here."

The hand
touches me slowly,
trembling with love, caresses
the thin recorded lines
of the memory,
sculpting my face,
with enormous effort.
In the tremoring
waves intensify.
Rays of love
stream from the hand
of my dying father.

Alien fingers
hold my hand,
move it to his
body that is already
on his way to Vega
or to the evening star.
Pain is a sign.
Starved eyes,
yearning for free space
farther up
where the signs disappear.

Point midnight.
Birth.
Without fear.

The Solitude of the Bee,
or Correspondence with Kappus

*For fame is ultimately but the summary of all misunderstandings that crystallize about a
new name. … they assembled about the name, not about the work—a work that has grown
far beyond this name's sound and limitations, and that has become nameless as a plain is
nameless or a sea that has a name but on the map, in books, and to men, but which is, in
reality, but distance, movement and depth.* —Rainer Maria Rilke

Prologue

You were happy that Christmas 1908
somewhere out of danger
courageous and alone in your raw reality.
I only know a few of your poems
and am very grateful for your letters to Rilke.
It's lovely to be neither complementary nor a border.
Is it of any significance whether one hundred years on
my questions are similar to yours?

The bee will die all because of my thin skin,
human skin.
Its sting is used to bears' muzzles
and furry bodies.

The danger that I will suffocate
because of my intolerance to the sting
—my old weakness—
has nothing to do with the bee.

Is all the horror in our dreams really only
our fragility calling out for help?

1.

those difficult moments of forlorn
familiar gestures and smells
the crossing of that threshold

our house changes when a guest arrives
bearing sword lilies of the nicest kind, politely
this arrival changes us before we ever meet
the visitor is already in the garden
will soon ring the bell

these days we rarely leave doors open

the griever's patience recedes

alone and alert
quiet, but yet still patient with the lilies' swords

2.

the cat does not expect my touch
assumes that we have distinct territories
that my scent is not that of a cat
and thankfully isn't wrapped up
with another cat's scent
she's happy to be stroked though
leaves her scent on my clothes
then burrows into my lap
to find herself there

and what we call fate
forces it way out from within
rather than forcing its way in from without
and when the cat flies to the top of the tree
her eyes dream of more than the bird she is hunting

3.

a lonely person builds for what later may be possible
there's a lot of space to build
because his neighbors are far away and few
and the spaces he crosses to meet them are large

oh, his face was that entire space
and if having faith in what emerges from me
doesn't mean my place among the others is assured
only that it has its own place
because the day falls from me before the verse
and I am close to things
as Rilke taught me to be
in the great pregnancy of chance

and just as the first human learned to speak
the way each of us speaks his first words
I will speak
and I am Adam
If we suppose he was the first

and Adam is pregnant
before he gives birth

and the nights are still nights
they are still here
here they are

4.

this love
the only one worthy of the name
the love slowly won
the love copied from the spiders' ability
to spin individual threads and entire webs
the love acquired from the pride of trees
who weep and warn one another
when a person bearing an axe approaches
the love that consists of two solitudes
protecting, bordering and greeting one another

our work is to love and die like that
our work is simple
why do we need so much homework

the hedgehog sniffs at the mist with a keen nose
and even keener spikes
when and how will he open his senses and stomach
his eyes
when and how and where, will it be here, now, not at all

5.

and I live the sting
live its questions
begin to love what I never saw
give in more and more to the questions without answers
and my metamorphosis into a question
this thin skin
is learning the patience
to accept the sting
and ensuing death as necessary

that and much more
has a lot to do with the death of the bee

with the death of the beekeeper, with the numerous diaries
with his love for the geckos
with the cancer
with his dying man's altered sense of smell
so that even the bees didn't recognize him
and he died without being stung

what could be worse than that

6.

this loneliness of the bee
but bees are not solitary creatures

immigrants invade the larvae
and the bee is maimed before birth
the hive dies together
not alone the loss of the sting

my grief is more than I can bear
like a century ago
and I have so many questions
how will we survive, doubly
sting-less, honey-less

how can I forgive myself for this lonely death
it might have saved an entire hive
from me
from me
like a field without flowers
like a human thin skin

7.

the concentration of the moment
like a sculpture
like the sculptor himself
absorbed in the moment
ruling over it
like a room, sunny and airy
a lot of air, and only chairs and a table
nothing else
just a table
a lot of chairs
and the joy of the day

8.

it's not that there is more beauty here
but there is a lot of beauty here
because there's a lot of beauty everywhere

and once again I can exchange glances with the child's
wise absence of comprehension
defenses and sympathy

the child covers bare legs
covers shoulders
with a piece of clothing
a gesture of fragile protection
against a dead bee
a bee without a sting
left behind in my skin

and tears flow slowly and happily down the child's cheeks

Epilogue

elegant high moment

and I separate myself simply
separate myself for the last time

like a leaf that will not be reborn in humus
like a rope that disintegrates
like a tear that dries up before it reaches the eye
like a perfectly formed steel bridge that separates itself
       from the shore

a leaf preserved in amber
a rope that learns to fly
a tear of joy

a bridge erects, rises up from the shore
outstretched, graceful, large
no longer a bridge
if somebody wishes to reach the shore, let them swim or fly

swimming moments, flying moments

beautiful

v.
Three Times Daily
Rhinoceros Bicornis

On the Shore, the Cell Harp

1

The white bodies of the apple blossoms relax in the grass.
Their breaths followed the fierce storm.
The sun fans shadows on the frost,
infinite doubts are allowed: birdsong all around,
the wind strums the harp of each cell.
Here poetry gathers rice seedlings, and here
begins the prosaic: the secrets of the authorities
are stronger than those of the atom.
In the North and the South—the same grief and worry
dressed in wood and metal.
What the West and the East have committed
is written on the pale moon,
but it's still not full.

2

Auntie, don't give your grandchild
salads next week.
The fields are infested with black light.
The old woman trusts her niece,
puts on her glasses, washes each lettuce leaf
thoroughly under running water.
The child should be safe.
Nothing bad must happen.

3

Unrepeatable is the charm
of each blossom and of each tsunami,
物の哀れ *mono-no aware,*
ephemeral beauty, cell-spell,
the dark of the pupils scatters into space,
the atoms never stop
playing the game of perfection.
The fear gathers splinters of hope,
rolls red suns and small shells,
autumn leaves and news from comets.
The human is perfect
only in the attempt to begin again.

4

There are thundering waterfalls, also silent ones,
known and unknown rivers that listen.
Haughty grasses flourish in shallow waters.
It's the tiny flowers that explore the chasms.
Calm down. Aesthetics will prevail
even in disaster areas.
We don't give up. The iris will come.
There they are—the floating bridges of the lotus.

5

On the hill of encounters
the evening sun asks for confidence.
The settlements were given sonorous names:
Funaoka, Fukiage, Ukishima, Fukushima.
After the Kogarashi forest comes the Yokotate,
which consists only of one tree. Stuffy air,
hopefully no rain will beat down soon.
海 の 見える 席 が あ り ま す か? *Do you want a table
facing the water?*, the waitresses used to ask.
Women are not allowed to clean up now.

6

Earth's shaken confidence
misdiagnosed as a waterquake.
Ocean walls test their force, leave
a field flooded with memories.
The love of those who remained becomes deeper.
All guardians of the storm bend their bows,
lined up in front of the palace in dress uniforms,
waiting for the last roar. More and more
the fire becomes capricious, born by the water.

Jonah and the Cigarette Smoke

We have eaten the shark.
Now he'll continue to chew us.
The fish filet was juicy, delicious.
It reminded of the belly of the whale
as it slid down our throats.
Jonah paid; we thanked him.

Then we started coughing, not
because of the fishbones. There
was smoke. Aboard the Moby Dick
nobody had heard of the shark or
the coughing. The hunting continued,
and Jonah went on smoking.

Joys and Jaws

Postcard paradise in Southeast Asia,
palms, sunshine, empty beaches,
radiated corals, wild genomes,
mutant sharks with only one fin,
anemones using wreckages as reefs,
remains of atomic bomb tests'
stormy passions, in the Pacific
Bikini is an island not your swimsuit,
a third of our Earth repairs itself
from the Caesium of the ungentle touch.

Homo Anthropocenus, Finder of a Lower Jaw

A man on the shore, and sand
as far as the eye can see, infinity
born by an unimaginable process.

But our slow violence rapes grains,
constantly bound in concrete,
forced into a solid state.

Naked dunes yearn for the beach,
but each new building swallows more sand.
We don't recycle materials from the destroyed.

New priests blow up balloons with lies,
measure the radiation of ruins in closed rooms
with low radioactivity to claim danger,

store in landfills and fill their pockets.
Sandless, deserted shores
and islands drawn in ideology.

Shores we could maintain, leave
the loose rock to them. Earth which will
soon be gone, trickles over human skin.

Grains in the mouth, gnashing teeth,
bleeding gums. It's good to remove
the wisdom teeth that often get infected.

The sand is a threatened species.
During the search for new pits
jawbones of a semi-developed species were found

that ran everything into the ground
and buried their heads
in the sand.

Record Heat

Windows break easily when the sluggish air
suddenly turns somersaults.
Devices and pines are equal
targets when lightning strikes.
Then the heat takes over again. Sweat pours,
flows in all directions over the burning mantle of the city.
The #metoo movement brings about a #metwo
in the language of some of my favorite
poets and thinkers who turn in their graves
because each movement turns out to be a standstill.
In the local gardens nimble red squirrels
are still enthusiastic early birds.
The gray manic American squirrels
have already taken Normandy.
Pine martens are in urgent demand, as well as
know-how about invasions. In the jumble
of hot air layers we overlook the danger,
distracted by the constructed dangers of another migration.
Earth has its rules and consults only the universe,
not us. We speak of a heat record,
only to report an outrage the next day.
Awake too late at night, we become sleepwalkers
who never wake. It might save us
to return to our dreams.

Bait

—for José F.A. Oliver

Maybe I am the bait.
There is no one else by this side of the canal.
Just one man stands on the Bosporus,
just the moon or the moonlight
chews at my thoughts behind the clouds.

The water smacks in between,
longs to have teeth, longs to have me,
becomes increasingly furious. Knives
flare. For the first time
I am afraid of water.

Pain drips off the sliced land.
All these blades in the water's mouth:
Peace never had a place here—
Istanbul, Tzarigrad, Konstantinopel,
human bait, Bosporus, Chang´e, Uydu,

Kamer, Ay, Mehtap, Lunata, slashed
history shrouded in fog, gathered pieces
plastic wrapped for unpacking. The head's
clouded like soft cheese. Brain is breaded
in eggs and flour just like everything else.

It's a childhood memory and tastes good,
more tender and gentle than roasted heart.
Heart should be fried instead of breaded.
What do I bait?
Every decision is self-robbery,

prevents all other decisions.
We see more clearly in black and white
and more nuanced in gray than color.
Every decision is life. Life is pure decision.
This couldn't be more banal.

And so I wonder,
when I sit on this Earth taking its words apart
to turn closeness into a human dimension,
nearness to intimacy,
who do we send ourselves to as bait
when we talk about the Bosporus now?

Sleepless

—for Dennis Maloney

Long sleepless nights, zero melatonin,
not allowed for sale in Berlin.
Chronic pain, but diclofenac
is not available in the U.S. without a prescription.
Both are correct, says my liver
even though vice versa is possible.
I still don't know anymore
what is good and what is not.
War is infinite and studying physics doesn't help
neither me nor the German chancellor,
doesn't even help the Canadian astronaut
who sings in outer space, has no inner fears
and repeats his song to dreamt perfection.
We all repeat.
We repeat wars, diseases.
We reiterate our desperation.
Dark matter is becoming increasingly fashionable.
Dark energy seems to get over that.
And I'm sleepless trying to understand
what isn't dark in the metaphor.
Faraway in Big Sur, a friend dreams
the dreams of my Kyoto friends,
and I'm in between, a sleepless princess
who has guarded the secret of peace
for one hundred years.

I teach about the story of killing
to the children from Kabul,
children in Berlin about the outcome
of a replacement war,
teach myself not to give up and to continue
to believe that humanity can—and so can I—
survive in this universe,
by rejecting all killing
and taking responsibility to overcome
the fear of death. I call on poetry for help
as in the Bulgarian fairytale the sons
called on trouble for such a long time
till they found their own way to go on.
And I do not cross borders
and do not help others to cross borders
because I don't understand where the sides are.
For me it's all one. And thus I walk
becoming myself a border, boundary, rim, edge,
a living line rejecting the whole concept of exclusion.
I am sleepless in a palace without a fence
and no roses, not hopelessly longing
to wake up through kisses.
One never wakes because of others.

Pledge

"What do you seek with that dagger? Speak!"
The angry voice challenged him.
"To free the city from the tyrant!"
—F. Schiller

Red colors penetrate Malta's winter.
Cactus blossoms, heather, and peppercorns
scatter among monumental white stones
and brightly painted porches; *kbir* and *gravi,*
the mighty fortress never despaired,
a rock and a boat, always hoping for peace
in the Mediterranean's heart.

In Syracuse, Pallas Athena shines
in the cathedral next to Our Lady.
Archimedes and Frederick the Great
haunt. The sea has belonged to Odysseus
ever since. Today border guards prevent
the waves from sending desert dust to land,
the winds blow saltier, and we pretend
that we believe in Europe's beginnings.

Three Times Daily Rhinoceros Bicornis

like when you are choking your mother, like when the daughter strangles her mother, because the men have blown themselves up with all of the children, like when the daughter tightens the thread around her mother's neck because fate has her hanging by a thread, a fate that was meant for another but became hers

like when shooting at the father, like when the son shoots the father, because three suicide bombers have become his fate, the fate of the son, even though that fate is not meant for anyone

like when a black rhino calls S.O.S., like when a black rhino calls because it cannot accept that its fate is already sealed, that man and animal die together, because the human likes to die, likes to bring others to death even more

like when it's prescribed, when it's been written in a prescription that taking rhinoceros bicornis three times daily leads to god, like when three times a week one suicide bomber is commended, like when someone believes that god could be reached by killing, that he exists, and that he issues prescriptions to kill

like when people think it's been prescribed, like when the humans think that killing is their fate

like when one is drowning children, when one is letting children drown at sea, like when one doesn't think about it much, like when one thinks about it yet simply looks on, like when one has thought, has looked, and now is no longer looking like when you are a woman, like when you're a woman and that doesn't make a difference, because the fate is the same, the fate of humankind, the story of the earth

like when strangling the mother, shooting the father, drowning the children, eradicating the rhinoceros and blowing oneself up helps you forget that god cannot help you

like when I am the one who is that human

like when I am not that one

I am not

VI
Anthroposcene

Adding a New Word to the Dictionary

Antroposcene [æn'θrɒpəˌseen], noun. A proposed term for the present epoch (from the time of the first discussion on the Anthropocene and onwards), during which humanity has begun to be aware of its own self-performance

Definitions:

    1 : a hyper-performative, quantitative, technology- and multiverse-oriented, image-driven period of a highly self-reflective and fully interconnected semi-educated humanity

    2 : a time of increased self-staging of humanity during the later Holocene

    3 : a striking process that takes place between humanity and Earth. Accidents, scandals, noisy wrestling between people and planet, emerging from despair when life-sustaining conditions erode

    4 : special venues in the solar system where a theatrical performance of living beings—who are capable to think, speak and have social life—is played

    5 : episodes in the divine universal art work with plot actions that unmask the politics of the invisible

    6 : fierce self-reproaches

7 : expressions of price, of human value, dependent on losses, profits and the interference with nature

8 : a psychological state in which humans are obsessed with fears and in order to escape from them again believe themselves to be the center of the universe and the purpose of the world's creation; this does not prevent them from destroying more than creating. Provoked by anthropocentrism, an unscientific, religion and idealism related doctrine

Word Origin: from anthropo- and –scene; from Old Greek (anthrō-pos) = human, Prefix, keyword in compositions meaning human; latin scaena, scena = locale, ancient greek σκηνή (skēnế) = tent, hut

First known use: Tzveta Sofronieva, Hochroth, March 2017

Deutsch: *Anthroposzene, die,* Wortart: Substantiv, feminin. Worttrennung: An|thro|po|sze|ne
Aussprache: [antʀopoˈsʦeːnə]
Synonym: Anthropozähne

български: антропоцена, антропосцена (цената и сцената на човека).

#kapustamaria

Kapusta Maria
Maria's cabbage
Kohl und Maria
Pusta Мария ex опустяла
зелева
зелена
зе-еее-ле Se-eee-le
cheeeese
cake Käse-kuchen
-füße a hegy lábánál
hegyes köröm hegyes mell
В полите на планината
politeia planinar
politena plan@a
oversized chromosome
Garten-Haar-Mücke
Kräuter Kröte Bäche
Bach Klang Wach—ach!
Maria Madonna mia

#instructionsforpicklingsauerkraut

There are many instructions for pickling sauerkraut
and other vegetables.

As Maria's mother used to say
be entertaining, and you can
easily survive the present.
Sauerkraut has a lot of vitamin C. It's good for you.
Red wine is good for you too,
and vinotherapy is good for your skin.

#marketnetbags

Market net bags are most convenient
for transporting cabbage
to prepare it for winter.

Nets emerge all the time
both female and male, intersex. We
mistakenly think nature
has hierarchy.
Forms, expressions, cooking recipes,
additional algorithms,
all rhythm
and nodes of associations.

A mountain is not always a part of a mountain chain,
but a mountain chain is a network of mountains,
and a forest is a network of trees.

A hill is not less of a mountain.
It's just another form of expression
for a curve in a landscape,
an expression of land, a line, an I,

ein Ausdruck des Landstrichs, ein Strich.
ein Ich, a Self in the Sauerkraut Recipes Study,
not necessarily gluten-free.

#mymothersdog

"My mother's dog was modern and funny.
He peed only in the designated places.
He was castrated and frustrated," Maria said.

kutyapisi пиши бриши l'etranger ширина
родината пасмина псета pesetta Euro Europe
rope and rape app тихо се сипе първият сняг
галено щипе всички ни пак, the puppy е още
малко кутре, може ли Шаро да разбере, колко си
глупав half-breed сега how anxious гледаш снега
visitor viitor gate of the genes megalomania megjelölni

> a dog's pee writes on the white, wipe the wide,
> learn to mop and to mob the migrant, mother
> tongue, father land, wolf pack, dogs in the manger,
> what a mess, hoggishness, human stress, decimal,
> euro in bar, rope and rape, be an ape, megastar,
> puppy dog, don't be pissed off with your first snow
> or dodge the frost, crossbreed, take a step, look ahead,
> downstage, mongrel, anxious eyes, ice's yours, so am I,
> being dogged, you crash into the gate, stay ahead
> of the pack, you're the genes' gatecrasher, a megahit,
> blast! brand: a human who hotdogs megalomania

#ascientificexplanationofterritory

A scientific explanation of the territory of dogs and wolves
and the biological meaning of peeing all over the place
is simple: in the peed circle only this male animal
can disseminate genetic information.

In these places, no matter what people would admit
or how often people pretended differently,
genetic purity has always been of great importance.

"But the rule is that men do not think, live, act like women, and
that's not just upbringing," writes *Brigitte* 2003 on page 246 in issue
5 or page 245 in issue 6. "It has something to do with the brain, the
bones, the genes, or whatever! As far as I am concerned also with
the fact that he can just pee in the open air on every tree and mark
the area ... This seems to provide a fatal self-confidence."

Shake a leg! Take a whiz!
Pinkeln! Tinkle!

Mark the stage!

The pee labeled circle
turns into
a strange
stage!

#onstagecatsalwayswin

On stage cats always win
Wildcats fascinate.
The lion as the king of animals,
the pride of creation,
is so similar to us, isn't he?
Wildlife videos on Netflix and YouTube
confirm the leading role of the I.S.:
On the stage, after the fight
the lion kills its rivals
and all male offspring,
rapes the daughters,
and lets the females hunt for food.

#sweetkittens

Sweet kittens!
Each one wants a tomcat.
Tomcat penises are spiked and
hurt. An ache is the alpha and omega
of the genetic cleansing

Boli-Liebe-Libo
Love Libido

pruning, mutilating, beating,
stoning, tormenting,
assassinating, cleaning.

#muhammadabrahamjesuschristbuddha

Muhammad, Abraham, Jesus Christ, Buddha,
Krishna, Baha'ullah, et cetera,
kings in the manger.
Mama mia, Mary, Mariaaa,
who was your son,
and why do you give birth
on stage
every year?

#stageddesire

staged desire backstage back pain sigh
painful fulltimejob munkahelyi ártalom harm
replacement bone replacement csontpótlás костен
мозък brainstorming буреносен облак над облаците
седмото небе felhőtlen a szeplőtlen ябълката
божие докосване или голямото инсцениране
constructing a part of the divine detail
a part of the whole chain load drawers боли

> staged desire, backstage, back pain, sigh,
> full-back, full-time job, fully replaced,
> substituted bone, marrow in bones, spinal
> cord, cordial drugs and cordial thanks,
> cordials in a brandy glass, belly brain,
> brain fog, bedlam storm, brainstorming,
> on seventh day be on cloud nine, there's
> a near-touching hand, great show, big shot,
> apple, constructing a part of the divine, taking
> apart, fragments loaded in drawers, it aches

#focusondetail

Focus on detail, forget the whole
if you argue about faith.

When we see the reproduction
of Michelangelo on a postcard from Rome,
we don't know it's about
the Three Levels of Existence.

Everywhere countless reproductions
of the near-touching fingers.
We see only two approaching hands,
we know nothing more, we don't know.
In the entire picture everybody is present
since Adam and Noah,
since the beginning of history until today,
until you and me.

In the Sistine Chapel in Rome we don't see
the image we know from the postcard.
Most of the things we misinterpret
because we're simply overstressed.

The surgeon sees a prolapse on the Roentgen
or in an MRI. Maybe the psyche is also depicted.
But he doesn't see all the organs
or the narrative of their infections and sorrows.

Quantum physics, nuclear spin, imaging,
a vertebra radiates, we see a detail and believe we know,
but we'd better study the genealogy of the waves.

People need to separate things
to be able to
find solutions,
and they believe these
solutions for eternity.

Zoom in.
Zoom out.

Distance instead of destruction.

#itsfuntogroupfoodtogether

It's fun to group food together
and combine the groups for nutrition,
more than combi vans, a broken down
van or a breakdown, a balanced diet,
and generally some balance,
helps to make one final choice,
aim, and shoot.

Treffen!
Les décisions ont
une odeur de géométrie.

Details and frames are both
satisfied.
Zoom in
and
out.

#thestageshines

The stage shines!
It's full of details.
Bravo, brava, bravi!
Брадви секат кости.
Bones and emotions
chopped with an ax,
taken apart, withheld,
separated, crushed,
stuck in different drawers,
locked
or consumed.

The curtain
opens and closes
at the same time.

#handsdegetkézfejдланиHaut

hands, deget, kézfej, длани, Haut
допир,
this touch, that death
for my ear
t, d and th do not differ
so tickle
tinkle the ivories
tingling with the fear of not hearing
year in yearning, sense in absence
as in asylum, some in awesome,
miss in mission, om in .com
lust in loss since lust in Verlust
long is the longing
to touch
interface manipulate detect distract
simulate feel faint
пръсти пет bet nets of neurotransmitters
touching skin evokes one
touching a key recalls another
mobile phone tablet hey ray player
black and white
laptop buttons
ivories on a grand piano

me
touching

#thestringsofthemultiverse

the strings of the multiverse
and the strings of guitars
do not differ
in our imagination
we need music
desperately
all this music   in the ghettos
all these colors   around the globe
all these smiles and tears   on the road
refugees meet   migrant-hunters
and the music   nonstop
a collision
noise   inside blood
rhythm in legs
in the penniless days
amidst cultural shocks
black white other and more
voices and fingers   voices and fingers
and the guitars are the same
red and electric ones
the hat of the singer
the guitarist's fingers
the pianist's forehead
the drummer's cheeks
my lips my pen   the heart of my hope
tangled in string theory   as an excuse

#thisdirtywordhope

This dirty word
Hope

When black white and all others
join in buses and subways equality comes
When Arabs and Jews
become citizens with respect for each other
war is over
When the Berlin Wall falls
no wall can divide
When voters vote
and know who to vote for
this means democracy

We've built this stage in order
to feed the people
but the stage must be fed with people
La guerre coupe le jardin, cyber arena
la façon dont nous vivons
At once actors and audience

#ontheearthssurface

On the Earth's surface
anthropoid teeth gnaw.
In the decisive scene
the background always shifts
into the foreground.

#thedirectorshoutsattheactors

The director shouts at the actors:
Make the holes in memory pictorially clear.

The signs of the dollar and the euro,
logos of TV channels, sheriffs,
pouring down sex bombs, flooded rooms, silk burkas
take the air away, thirst,
local artificially-produced water
after a food technology recipe, *bon*
aqua

Toast your bun
genetically designed
of course (finally, this soy flour comes from the U.S.,
FOR US)

and organize your brain structures
for maximal use.
الاستغلال
Distribute goods and truth
Ware vera моята вяра в дните chestiti wahrer Ver-Trieb
This
Tribute
Dos, tres … uno!

But please,
PLEASE!
Use more symbols,
more images.

Not these words!

#alanguagelesson

A language lesson:
Go! Six two three! And
tres dos uno:

Am I a singer?
Yes, you are.

Are you a writer?
Yes, I am.

The singer sings songs.
The writer writes books.

The songs are to be heard.
The books are to be read.

She can hear songs online.
He can read books online.

We can buy songs online.
They can buy books online.

Why don't we take a shower?
Is it time to take a shower?

Yes, it is.

#andyoumayfindyourselflivinginashotgunshack

And you may find yourself living in a shotgun shack,
and you may find yourself in another part of the world
with some   TALKING HEADS
freestyling o n c e   i n a l i f e t i m e .
And you may ask yourself: Am I right? Am I wrong?
And you may say to yourself: What have I done?
And you may tell yourself: It's all right.
And you may ask yourself: How do I know?
Everything's stuck together.

```
E | 5-5-5--2--5------------- |
B | 5-5-5--3--5---3--3-3--3- |
G | --------------2--2-2--2- |
D | ----------------------- |
A | ----------------------- |
E | ----------------------- |
```

A F# F#m A
A F# F#m A
A F# F#m A
A F# F#m A
     F#m A F#m
A A F#m F#m A
F# G F# G
F# G F# G

What's the matter with you?

It's alright.
How do you know?

How do you know
which choice explodes in your soul,
which thunderstorm has passed within you
and how far it is?
Glaciers turn into salt,
a sand-cheek warms your hand
and clings to you.
How many grit wounds
on hands and faces, and on hearts
are yet to come?

Until the supercell turns into sand.
Same as it ever was.

#toomanycatsarebeingmanipulated

Too many cats are being manipulated
as if they were Erwin Schrödinger's cats,
parallel universes feed scripts,
but few of us understand how GPS works.
More and more schools are teaching creationism
in place of Darwin.
We, humans, fear ourselves. And you and me?
For two lives' time we seek the source
to throw in our words,
to let them swim together,
to wring them out
and drink.

#christmaseveamanger

Christmas Eve, a manger
пещерата, както я знаем as usual,
now completely empty.*

All expelled.
Only donkeys and sheep,
soon they'll not be there either.

---

* "During the last century, Jews were persecuted, and not only then. They were exterminated. Jesus, Mary and Joseph were Jews too. That's why they're missing. Also exiled are the Arabs, the Wise Men—one of whom is from Ethiopia, Africa, looking for sanctuary all over the world. The shepherds are Palestinians; they too are not to be seen there. Later, Jesus, Mary and Joseph fled from Egypt to escape the mindless rage of a human king; they were refugees. There are so many of them today. This is what the world looks like today on the birth of Jesus Christ 2016: the birth without Jews, without Arabs, without Africans, without refugees. What will be left of the manger this year? Only the donkey and the ox, and maybe some sheep." (Excerpt from the Christmas Eve service message in Sofia)

#withhangingtongues

With hanging tongues the great ones pant after sausages
in the name of fatherland, freedom and democracy.
The lesser ones snoop on the Anthropocene.
The ordinary people pay taxes and tickets,
and sometimes manage to snap up a sausage too.
The newcomers bring even more hunger.
In the bistro of the theater, foreign specialties are offered,
also Arab and Balkan food, a selection of sheep cheese
and yogurt started with Western cultures.
"They will kill each other with this fanaticism
and even blow us up," the waiter says to my colleague,
a historian who cuts meat on a spit and
unburies vegetables served in a clay pot.
He dines with pleasure, as if there were
no spectacle beforehand and no intermission.
The stage designer,
hostile because of the only local power outage since '45,
gobbles a wienerwurst quickly and hurries back
to the technical desk.
In the second act, it becomes clearer and clearer:
Love between people from different nations
is in direct correlation with love between people and sausages.

#libertyissosureofherself

Liberty is so sure of herself as a statue
in New York's harbor. The ferry transfers
passengers just below her nose. They
read in newspapers about Prague, the fall
of the Berlin Wall, and sometimes about Panama.
But there's never coverage about the Native Americans.
Divorce rates and abortion are often discussed.
The sleepy passengers—it's late
to head home (just like in "Working Girl,"
the Hollywood movie, don't you remember?)—
throw away their newspapers in the garbage bins
right at the ferry's door. The day is over.
And the statue is so well lit
that it's obvious: Inside it's empty.

That was back in 1989. Now the ferry
is lit by hundreds of Smart- and i-Phone screens,
minds and hands twitter.
Liberty is not so sure anymore.

#breakup

BREAK-UP
DESINTEGRATION

	WHAT IS	
	THE USE OF	falling in love
with your-self	GAINING	to be more- most-
having believed in	THE WHOLE	humanity in the
bottomless hell	WORLD	
	IF	I win it will
be for all for	YOU	but is it normal to
	LOSE	
to deny	YOURSELF	
	?	
	YOUR SELF	-security -fishness
	SELF	-awareness -existence
	SELF	-creating -consciousness

203

To rest my head in your lap,
just to sit near you for a while
in the chaos, in the madness of this place
everyone tries to save themselves
but our salvation passes through others,
an instinct for self-preservation when there's rumbling
before an eruption is
coming, the summer is coming,
the heat when the new diary of dreams will be written,
and disturbed insane eyes do not stop to pray
for rain, for good days
on the boundary of death,
could we not at least overcome
our tiredness of ourselves?

#terraincognita

Ter

Terra ——Earth, we may not say it was ours.

Terrain –preparation for a new activity, for constructing.

Territory – to be won, inhabited, conceived, given up and so on.

Terrier -– dog breed (so far known used only in this context).

Teror – a water source on Gran Canaria, quenches the thirst of
        locals and tourists.

Ror

Raw meat and raw fish are called sashimi, carpaccio or mett
depending on the type of animal and food preparation.

R.o.r. means released on recognizance,

Ro-Ro is a roll-on roll-off ship, where vehicles can be driven on,
so rain can be avoided. One can eat sashimi in peace.

Ist

Yes it is, and it's part of the publicist, Polizist, futurist, machinist,
communist, columnist,
ne bis in idem.

In German there is
In

Inn is a river, connects Tyrol with the Black Sea;
the in-side is the opposite of the outside,
and also "it's in" and "it's in to be in."
Behave yourself post-modern, post-futurist,
post-anthropocene.

Ter-ror-ist-in. Does a female terrorist,
declare that being a terrorist is in?

Worlds and words. Am I a terrorist
in the Terra Incognita of Language?

Walking the narrow ridge of the knife's edge:
if you go right — man's world,
to the left — anti-man.
proceed deeper — it cuts you,
if you jump — it halves you.
Careful, slow, thoughtful, motherly, patient, forgiving,
loud, between T, R and S, and without A, certainly without A
and for sure without Z.

#weneednowadictionarypoem

We need now a dictionary poem, and I fish for one.

Let us start Fishing 1614 to end 2014 (Six hundred sounds good
and we should always keep a frame, shouldn't we?):
There is no F so good as in troubled waters.
No F to the Sea, no Service to the King.

What is all this F about when there is nothing? Take an F-basket
under the arm or better an F-box so arranged that a fish going into
it can't get out.
At night the shore was brilliant with the F-lights in the canoes.
They seemed to be on a F-expedition. The F-frog grows to a large
size. They are not true F-hawks, after all. The solitude was broken
by the plaintive scream of the F-eagles.

She was F around in the cupboard for a plate.
I wish I had the F of your back that is so bent.
You can be F for a compliment by saying "And how does my outfit
look today?" That's fishy.

He threw out two or three F-questions. And somewhere in between
we realized that [1884, Mark Twain's Huck Finn, xxxvii. 376] we
curled him up like an F-worm.

And a lot of F in Fishing of F -bark, -basket, -boat, -box,
-compromise, -craft, -expedition, -gear, -ground, -hook, -house,
-hutch, -light, -limit, -line, -net, -party, -pen, -port, -rights, -season,

-ship, -smack, -spear, -tackle, -town, -trade, -trip, -village, -weir, -worm, F -admiral, -breeze, -crib, -flake, -float, -pole, -tool, -tube, -wand, -rod, -key, -plate, -frog, -eagle, -owl, -hawk, F -planet, -adventure, -experience, -lines, -lures, -reels, -supplies, -simulator, -equipment, -shop, unlimited,

Total F, freshwater F, F for information, F for affection.

It all suggests that you're looking for something without always knowing precisely what it is.

Normal F (with a hook and rod) is the action, art, or practice of catching any of the various cold-blooded, aquatic vertebrates, having gills, commonly fins, and typically an elongated body covered with scales; to secure (an anchor) by raising the flukes; to reinforce (a mast or other spar) by fastening a spar, batten, metal bar, or the like, lengthwise over a weak place.

F can be also another word for piscary. We know that F-rod (1550s) is older than F-pole (1791). You are certainly F when you draw or search through.

By F with your hands you might not be looking while you're feeling for something.
Hunting and F to hone the skills my father and grandfather passed on to me.
[O]f all diversions which ingenuity ever devised for the relief of

idleness, F is the worst quality to amuse a man who is at once indolent and impatient. [Scott, *Waverly*, 1814].

To go F: to undertake a search for facts, esp. by a legal or quasi-legal process like a grand jury investigation [*American Slang*, 4th Edition, B. A. Kipfer, Ph.D. and R. L. Chapman, Ph.D.,© 2007 by HarperCollins Publishers]. The second definition here is important. To be F for something can mean to try and get information out of somebody but not by asking for it directly, i.e., by asking leading questions; and to select a microscopic object in a fluid; or to rob on the highways (pronounced the same way as F): the fraudulent practice of sending emails purporting to be from reputable companies to induce individuals to reveal personal information, such as passwords and credit card numbers, online.

Using bait in an attempt to catch a victim. Attack, manipulation, clone, link, filter, threat, invasion, technique, hacker, cover redirect, social engineering: I really hear F in phishing!
And let us enjoy all the F in Zwiebelfische und frische Zungenbrecher like

Fischers Fritze fischt frische Fische Frische Fische fischt Fischers Fritze.

Long live dictionaries! Vives les poèmes!
Vive l'anthroposcène!

#dearsadones

Dear sad ones in the evening when you put out the lights or candles near your beds, if you ever had them. Dear tired ones who don't want to read anything noble and prefer to exchange news and sauerkraut recipes, who are thinking about humanity and where we are going, eternal migrants, scattered on the map of the universe that turns, and with it turns our Earth. Every exit from orbiting is dangerous. With each attempt to get out of the tumult we get closer to danger and to ourselves.

I write to you far away from prestigious stages.

I give you my books.

I read to you on the coast, by the riverside, in small city cafes, in post offices, classrooms, laboratories, in the middle of potato fields, in Mabelle's house with her children, in meadows along mountain trails.

Soft and gentle are the waves of poetry.

VI
Wonder Detector

Dusting, Waste Disposal

Clouds of gas, vapor, haze, dust, fog, stars,
unification of empty universes, expansion,
swift, urgent, determined, hastily, future-
oriented, unimaginable, simultaneous, birth
of a radioactive force, helium from hydrogen,
constant fusion, heavy elements in the core,
dying suns, explosions of stars, awesome new
worlds, waves of attraction, dust from light
carries everything in a net of understanding.
Stars to ashes, ashes to earth, earth to dust,
dust to man, dust, too much dust.

Infrared camera, thousands of degrees,
simulation of the beginnings
to understand and endure ourselves, at first
everything must crust, cool down, but it's raining
meteors, movement becomes heat, fire, primeval
waiting, lava only becomes rock when it's cold,
really cool, doesn't give a damn, clearly modern.
Hidden, virtual water, vapor, at first vapor,
then oceans, still poisonous, afterward hardworking
bacteria that discharge garbage: OXYGEN.
Will our waste ever be of such value?

The Fourth Dimension

in the slow violence against rivers and oceans
the responsibility of humans for themselves is missing
we are younger and lazier
bacteria do not consider themselves the elite
they have no fear and need no faith
that lets them assume they are special

they take care of us
their vehicles for gene exchange
clear away the remains we amass
they endure us as if we were a volcano
that for a short time
wraps everything in dust and twilight

they relentlessly loosen lava rock
mix fossil DNA with the living
they rebuild time
the elderly ones since 250 million years
perhaps in the fullness of time reaching grand age
we also will embrace the fourth dimension

More Future

Present: starting position

The skies are pierced
by the eyes of telescopes
and the anxiety of mobile phones.
We haven't yet found dumps for the inherited
garbage of crashed satellites, but we persistently
scout the relationships of binary stars
and pry into who goes into gravitational holes
to fertilize the universe.
We discover a planet that resembles ours,
X million light-years away, with water
and temperatures between 30 and 100 degrees.
We find fungus spores in the clouds
of interplanetary spaces. Emotions
are modulated every day in our hearts,
and I'm not sure if this hurts the skies
or if they enjoy it.
I simply continue to write letters, but
I'm certainly not sending them to aliens,
not yet, not today.

Future 1.
First possible future

World's resurrection
from trash
Methanogenic archaea
Plastic-eating creature
Natural stock
Anachronic
Other evolution

Future 2.

There are no pink elephants,
I say soberly
and immediately imagine
a pink elephant.
I am human.
Unable to survey
the consequences
of my actions.
Unwilling to admit failure.
Able. Willing.
A new evasion from knowledge
seems imminent.

Future 3.

We need repetition,
we're in need of another moon,
we carry the necessity of inventing
an outer-space-bike
that we can ride on two lunar wheels
longing to emigrate
to a place where there's only one moon.
And we need
to tell someone about all of this.

Future 4.

We strive to survive.
This endeavor eludes us:
many unknown variables,
hardly clear constants. Safe
method: less consumption
would help us work out the task.

Future 5.
An original version of future

Stages of Matter:

Big Bang egg.
Through fire inorganic and unconscious.
Through water organic and unconscious.
Through language organic and aware.
Through knowledge artificial intelligence,
organic and inorganic cyborg.
Growing up, finding a loophole in the mask,
complete transformation to imago.
Fully inorganic and very conscious.

So God becomes it-her-him-self,
sorts it-her-him-self out
after we have created it-her-him,
after it-she-he created us.

We are God
as a larva.

Future 6.
Coming from the past and translated once more

But if you realize that he was not in your childhood, and not before, if you suspect that Jesus Christ has been deceived by his yearning and Muhammed betrayed by his pride—and if you feel with horror that he is not even now at this hour, when we speak of him—what is it that entitles you to miss him, who never was, like a past man, and seek as if he were lost?

Why do you not think that he is the Coming One to come from eternity, the future, the finite fruit of a tree whose leaves we are? What is stopping you from throwing off his birth into the ages to come, and to live your life as if it were a painful and beautiful day in the story of a great pregnancy? Do you not see how everything that happens is always a new beginning, and could it not be his beginning, since beginning in itself is always so beautiful? If he is the most perfect, must not everything before him be less, so that he may choose from abundance and opulence? Does he not have to be the last one who will embrace everything, and what sense would we have if the one we were asking for had already been?

Be patient and willing, and think that the least we can do is not to make his genesis more difficult than the earth makes it to the spring when it wants to come.

And be happy and confident.

Yours
Rainer Maria Rilke
December 23, 1903

Future 7.
Perhaps a reality

Aliens—
A. come and help
B. come again and destroy
C. come and cause something in between
D. do not come

The autochthonous
backbone
is often a subject of examination.

Future 8.
Another variation

A meteor kiss, a sneeze of the sun
and we are dust for others,
as when at the court of peace
bodies become earth, ash or plankton.
Rickettsia, rockets, spacetime—
what's the difference for us?
Everything is just normal, takes its course,
whatever we consider normal.
We constantly just want too much.

9th chance for a future

Geologically only a layer of processed material will remain,
bits of inorganic stuff, some concrete rubble, but acid
will decompose these as well, a small cemetery of rare earth
metals perhaps, ordinary dust sedimentation, the keyword for it:
mega-volcano. We assumed the right to shape the earth,
but we are not the future of the Earth's strata.

It's about us now, and directly about the future of our children.
It's about beauty continuing to exist as we know it and life
still full of colors. It's about sensing snow, touching skin,
watching whales and dolphins, bees, tasting honey, flying
with birds, sailing in the wind, breathing.
Can we finally open hearts and eyes instead of mouths?

Most likely unescapable future

Skyscrapers, full of folded fruit fields.
Rainforest avenues in garden history museums.
Salts for a clean tiny sea in the tub.
Wrapped scented reminders of flowers.
Graphic art of decayed bird feathers.

Future after the three seconds
that our brain can supposedly feel as present:

A smell of split wood, freshly-brewed tea,
a poem, a friend,
a vision, crisp air,
fulfilled dreams, new dreams,
and back to work.

Elementary Needs

Raw materials in the focus of the sun,
photon bombardment on rock.
A flood of light evaporates everything,
makes way for more than one god.
Jupiter pulls back and Earths,
Neptunes, Mercuries are born, and so on.
Gaia will need Mary later on,
and Luna,
the moon is probably bisexual.
The main point is that it's a companion.
Then main thing is
that the tumbling gets tamer,
turns into attraction, breathable air.
Storms become more and more violent.
Stabilize, stabilize.
Loneliness brings death.
Everyone needs a companion
and a free horizon.
It can't be done alone.
(Apollo 17, Houston.
It's still too early for that.)
Time is running out.
Come, stabilize,
give birth or collide
with another body.
From the debris of the union
a new partner will emerge.

And finally the embrace
of two dancers in harmony,
then new steps.
One body chooses the distance,
provides the necessary stability.
Trial and error,
the relationship's fine tuning,
complex and frightening.
Sun, moon and stars,
without them no Earth,
no lanterns and rebirth.
Sonne, Mond und Sterne,
Ohne sie keine Erde,
keine Kinderlaterne.
Laterne, Laterne
Sonne, Mond und Sterne.
A lucky variety of coincidence
that saves us.

The Dark (Loutrophoros)

1 : rim - 2 : neck - 3 : handle - 4 : shoulder - 5 : belly or body - 6 : foot

The dark in the pupils
is the same as the dark
between the stars. It
soaks everything up,
can accept everything,
transform
everything,
is the deepest
origin,
a prerequisite
for the genesis
of life. Deep,
manifold,
narrow passages,
tight, cloudy,
murky, we belong somewhere
else, we belong to
a later era. Always liquid
water, water that is not yet
clouds, ice or steam,
water as we like to
drink, as living
water, just like
that. We need this
information.

In the space of the dark
many questions remain:
Where did the cloud go? How
did we get out of the cloud?
At first drop like a stone, then
as water. Oh, how many
more skills should a woman have?

Strong Interaction

Преблизко си. Jestem blisko,
za blisko, żeby mu się śnić.
You are too close to me in your sleep.
You are dreaming of the gas station attendant
who gave you the fuel that you call dark energy
and think you need more urgently than ever.
You are dreaming of the waitress
who served you the coffee,
which you call dark matter and devour
believing you achieve inner cohesion.
You're dreaming next to me
in our marital bed, more honest than
those of love affairs inside hotels.
The interaction force puzzles our bed.
Closeness and attraction are a weak duet.
The larger the distance between the quarks,
the stronger the force between them.
"All quark and baloney," you say.
"So far free quarks haven't been observed."
You smack your lips in your sleep.
Your hand feels my shoulder, my hip.
You make love to me while I'm almost asleep
and beset by doubts about closeness,
having no dreams, while I believe in emptiness
which we always have to fill, each time anew.

In memory of Wisława Szymborska and Blaga Dimitrova

Tremors

It's shaking again in Turkey and Italy, in Indonesia.
Continental plates caress each other,
measure their strength
so to speak, not only politically,
but I prefer to define
in a feminine way.

The Canary Islands will soon break loose
to love the Statue of Liberty.
Quaking is mainly a matter of Earth,
but the filth in the water and air
is purely caused by us.
We enjoy and tend to suicides.

In our own tower of fog
we do not see far.
Maybe birds and photons
will show us the direction
and teach us to fly
without fears and machines.

Partake

1

Living fossils
horseshoe crabs resemble us
in development, their
childhood lasts twelve years

resurrecting
ancestors of the spiders that survived
the dinosaurs on the seabed
due to us a dying breed

their bodies are covered with eyes
like Indian deities
five pairs on their backs
to them the ultraviolet is visible

light receptors in the tail
recognize the difference
between shore and depth
the shift of the sea border

2

Ornate patterns
mystery of genesis
copyright of the sea
geometry genius blowfish

incessantly leading
to the center of love
generous radial forms
weeds are removed

fanning oxygen
over the children
what if we could do
something like that too

in Japan they've attempted to form
these kind of sand gardens for centuries
all that we can imagine in the arts
has already been created

3

Tides testify on the movement
of every border
a compensation of losses by
the sheer number of possibilities

magnetic seventh sense
dead volcanoes, deeper
waters, edges of reefs
surge of waves, jaws, digestion

compressed foreign skills
biology meets geology
electricity of fear
pulse, a cry of the heart

Wonder Detector

Detector of dark matter. Homo ludens loves
toys, plasma balls, flashes of light, embracing,
gravity turns galaxies into universes,
so teamwork plays a role after all.

We constantly prefer to play against each other.
Soon we will face a switch in the game
but exactly when is ninety-five percent secret.
So secrets frame our world after all.

It's all drifting apart, curiosity and dark ambition
are driving it, still everything stays connected,
embedded in the dark substance of our wishes,
documented by the aesthetics sensor.

Set of Possibilities

And for a while I'm Schrödinger's cat too
or occasionally Erwin himself, his mind's reflection,
the empty space that isn't empty or cannot be,
the forms in which it's worded,
their reasons to be that way
in the deep tribulation of their own time.
I recall diversity more than uniqueness
even if they don't contradict each other,
as if I were the creator of loneliness
presumptuous of the sun that created them.
The resentment of the sun to the light, to itself,
to the blinding bright past when everything
or at least a lot has started.
Time doesn't wipe away our tears,
time doesn't heal anything.
Time is just a dimension of our dreams.
Alleged causes. Escape.
The tired moons under my eyes
reveal the ghostly origins of the sun.

Multiverse seems attractive to you, but nature
knows neither majority nor multi-consciousness.
We believe that we have to discover everything.
But what is life? What are we, and what is our
free will? Every possible outcome exists
in its own universe. Multiverse is our inability
to understand through words, to shape with language.

We have not found anything more since.
We celebrate quantum theory and DNA,
and how amorous senses and thinking fortify each other,
which we do not admit or recognize
but rather avoid for convenience.
The World Wide Web lets us live
visually and sensually connected. Each day
becomes more technical, much more sensual.
We have bombs, energy, genetics,
a multiverse of responsibilities.
We have a lot of dangers
that are our own fault
and others that are not.
We will not be here for long.
But we have unlimited sets of possibilities
to experience.

Author's Notes

I have chosen *Multiverse* as the title of this volume because this notion from cosmology mirrors my poetics. On first glance it might be associated mainly with multilinguality, but it's far beyond: it is deeply related to the structure and the imaginary in my poetry and corresponds to the contemporary era in the visual arts and the natural sciences. In my work, a monolingual poem, a multilingual poem, a self-translation, a new version, a clone and an other-verse (alterverse) differ substantially.

I write poetry now predominantly in German, but I have written poems in Bulgarian since my early childhood, and I have occasionally written poems in English. A few of my poems were composed in different languages simultaneously and have versions in the three languages. Some are written purely as multilingual and include more languages. And I create poems that alternate without being versions or alternatives but happen simultaneously. I write these poems—in different languages and in different times, with different histories and higher-dimensional extensions—as other-verses (alterverses) and clones thus enlarging my space-time of poetry that is, itself, a language.

Many of my poems were translated from one of the three languages to another by professional translators or by native-speaking poets, and I have made several translations of my poems between the three languages. In my work with translators and with editors in these three languages, I have persistently conversed and thank my translators and editors in Bulgarian, English and German for their love and patience. For me my poems are not German, English or Bulgarian; they are Tzveta Sofronieva's poems. I also thank my translators and editors working beyond these three languages for their deep understanding of my work.

In this volume I include self-translations and other forms of my poetic. New versions are edited and slightly modified poems with the same original. Clones refer to the cell concept of the word as coming from the same gene but being fully different beings, as well as to the multiple existence of the same matter as a wave and particle in the manifestations of the same electron. Alterverse emerges when a strong diversion in the poetic theme occurs, together with a change in the observation and time dimension. The latter two forms can occur also in monolingual work but in the multilinguality manifest more clearly. Creating them is not a self-translation: It is a process of giving birth to a different poetic world.

I come from an old Slavic language written in the letters of Cyril—who in the 9th century argued with the Pope that Christianity could be preached in every language—and from a birthplace that accepts a multilingual existence as the most natural, as described by Bulgarian-born novelist and Nobel Laureate in Literature Elias Canetti in his autobiographical book *The Saved Language.* I studied with Joseph Brodsky and as a child already knew many interculturally working poets. Multilinguality is natural to me. My deep work in natural sciences since I was fourteen years old and my appreciation for the quest in science and poetry that for me are naturally so similar developed my poetics. As the cosmologist George Ellis comments, "The contemplation of the multiverse is an excellent opportunity to reflect on the nature of science and on the ultimate nature of existence: why we are here..." *(Scientific American,* "Does Multiverse Really Exist?") I feel that I am a tenant, and I deeply believe that this is what we all are. It is the interplay between our decisions and the coincidences or accidents in the self-organization of matter that counts.

"The most beautiful thing we can experience is the mysterious: it is the source of all true art and all science. He to whom this emotion is a stranger, who can no longer pause to wonder and stand rapt in awe, is as good as dead: his eyes are closed." – Albert Einstein.

Hurricane in Mesembria

The poems in this section originated during 1981-1990. They were written in Bulgarian except the few English originals.

"I or Cloning" is the fourth poem as alterverse (from 2019) of the poem "I" (from 1981) and is published here for the first time after the Bulgarian "Аз" in 1994, the German "Ich" in 2013, the British "Cloning" in 2019. The four poems develop a theme with meaning and imaginariness that differs much. In Bulgarian, the poem works with the words *азът* [azat] (English: the self) and *азот* [azot] (English: nitrogen) and focuses on the relationship between a growing up individual and society; it talks about loneliness and choices under dictatorship. The German poem works with the word *Stoff* (English: matter, material) in *Stickstoff* (nitrogen) and the invented words *Stich-Stoff* (piercing matter), *Ich-Stoff* (I-matter), *Erstick-Stoff,* (suffocating matter) and focuses on the pain in recognizing ourselves as migrants in nature. The British poem as other-verse works with splitters of many I's (plural), and focuses on the search for the Other in a globalized time-space with a large number of dimensions (as in String Theory). The poem here combines the previous in meaning and develops farther toward rebuilding human identity in the current era of the Anthropocene and understanding time as a many-branched tree, wherein every possible outcome is possible.

The epitaph is from *The Death of the Beekeeper* by the Swedish poet and novelist Lars Gustafsson (1936 – 2016). The central theme in this highly innovative book is revealed by the repeated motto of the protagonist: "We never give up. We begin anew." I read this book in 1978 as a high school student and subsequently spent all my breakfast money to buy copies of it for my friends. I am happy that I could meet the author in person and become friends with him in his later years.

"Perestroika Beach Carnival or The Great Salvation" and **"An Evening before Bulgaria's First Democratic Election"** mirror a time when the reforms towards liberalization—social, political and economic—in the Eastern Bloc started with Mikhail Gorbachev's reform program in the Soviet Union called Perestroika. In November 1989 demonstrations on ecological issues were staged in Bulgaria, and these soon broadened into a general campaign for political reform. In February 1990 the Communist Party, forced by street protests, gave up its claim to power. In 1990 the first free, openly-contested multi-party election in Bulgaria since 1931 was

240

held, won by the Bulgarian Socialist Party—the new name of the Communist Party. Much more time must pass before we can really look back to the seduction and lies during this period of change and bring this in a non-superficial way into literature.

"Hurrricane in Mesembria" and **"The Well-Disposed Week"** are included here in translation by Chantal Wright from my German versions of the Bulgarian originals.

Mesembria is the ancient name of the Bulgarian city of Nesebar on the Black Sea coast.

Anna Akhmatova (1889-1966) was one of the most significant Russian poets of the 20th century. She was highly admired by the Russian-American poet and Nobel Laureate for Literature Joseph Brodsky (1940-1996). I participated in Brodsky's master class in poetry in the U.K. in 1992.

Shopping and Fucking is a 1996 play by English playwright Mark Ravenhill which explored what is possible if consumerism supersedes all other moral codes.

"Journey to the West" was inspired by the poetry of the Canadian poet Margaret Atwood, whom I am delighted to know personally from when I first arrived in Canada in the late summer of 1989.

"Sometimes" was originally written in English on Christmas Eve of 1990 when, as a fellow in the Deutsches Museum in Munich, I was listening to the last recording by the self-taught American jazz pianist and singer Sweet Emma Barrett (1897 – 1983) in the home of German immunologist and pianist Rudolf Wank (1939-2017). It was written as a Christmas present for this beloved friend and his family.

"In times of Rain" was written in exile in Toronto, Canada, in 1989. Georgi Markov (1929 –1978) was a Bulgarian dissident writer who after his defection from the People's Republic of Bulgaria in 1968 lived in London and worked as a broadcaster and journalist for the BBC World Service and for the U.S.-funded Radio Free Europe. He used such forums to conduct a campaign of sarcastic criticism against the incumbent Bulgarian regime. Georgi Markov was assassinated on a London street via a micro-engineered pellet containing ricin, fired into his leg from an umbrella wielded by someone associated with the Bulgarian Secret Service and KGB.

"Homesick" is a clone of the "Homesick for Munich" poem written 1989 in Chicago in a telegram form. At the time I wrote "Homesick for Munich" I had not lived in Munich yet but connected this city with the rich traditions of Central and Western Europe. In this volume I have chosen the form in lines and have a different beginning, and I also took the last sentences out: I composed a new poem because the artificial features I was struck by back in 1989 in the U.S. have since spread to Europe and elsewhere. The poem in this volume does not refer to tradition or place, but to coming back to oneself. The change of the title was natural.

"Interference Pattern" is a new English poem related to the poem "Вина"(Guilt) from 1990. **"We Were Not Cavalry Horses"** is a poem about the oppositional writer's circles around the Bulgarian *samizdat* journals *Мост* (Bridge) and *Глас* (Voice), since some of their members had before or after the revolution compromised with non-democratic power structures. Here it is included as a translation from the Bulgarian.

"Captured in Light" was written in 1991 in Berlin in English and Bulgarian for my future husband. We spoke only in English since back then I did not speak any German. It was first published in 1992 with the title "Homeland" because for me it was a poem about language as the poet's only real home. When the poem was translated into German in 1996, I changed the title to "Captured in Light" because this was how I felt in the German culture back then: The German *Heimat* (homeland) was not a word that one could use in the way I used it in my poem because it carried the connotations of the Nazi use. This made me initiate and develop in the 1990s and the 2000s *Forbidden Words / (M)other Words* —a network of literary and academic projects, dealing with the memory of words, the power of linguistic memory in the communication between different cultures and the insights into language offered by multilingualism. The poem was slightly edited for rhythm and clarity.

Intersection Graph

Most of the poems in this section are written in the 1990s, including **"Conversation"** from January 28, 1996. The epitaph in the latter is from the 1980 autobiographical poem by the Russian-American poet Joseph Brodsky. Like him, I was "strongly advised" to emigrate from the Soviet Bloc and was in exile in the United States, fortunate to be able to give talks and do research with the support of historians of science in universities. Before, as a student in Bulgaria, I had read Brodsky's forbidden poetry in my teachers' retyped manuscripts of his Russian poems.

The last two poems in this section are exceptions in its time scale.

They were written in the Villa Aurora in California in 2005. I adopted German as my poetic language and since 2005 began actively writing in it. I had only occasionally written poems in German before then. In my essay "Un-lost in translation" (In *Shoreless Bridges*, Ed. E. Agoston-Nikolova, New York: Rodopi, 2010) I write about the process of adopting a literary language and about the "nationality of a poem."

The epitaph to **"Terminology"** is directly related to the definition of feminism in *Science and Gender* by the acclaimed U.S. scholar Evelyn Fox Keller, whom I got to know personally in 1990.

"The Mountains, a Man, a Woman" is the second part in my series of poems about a woman in a space parallel to *The Old Man and the Sea* by Ernest Hemingway. I have addressed the gender bi- and multilinguality as a challenge in all periods of my writing.

"Happiness after Reading Schopenhauer, in California" from 2005 was written in a beach café at the crossroads of Sunset Boulevard and Highway One. Arthur Schopenhauer (1788 – 1860) was a German philosopher and polyglot who has influenced thinkers and artists throughout the centuries, among others Goethe, Erwin Schrödinger, Albert Einstein, Jorge Luis Borges, and Samuel Beckett. For Schopenhauer, human desire was futile, illogical, directionless, and so all human action in the world caused suffering; a temporary way to escape this is through aesthetic contemplation.

Un-Lost in Translation

This section includes poems from 2007 to 2012.

The italicized German text in **"A Hand full of Water"** is taken from Wilhelm Müller's (1794–1827) poem "Das Wandern ist des Müllers Lust," which was set to music by Franz Schubert in the song cycle *Die schöne Müllerin*. The italicized Bulgarian text is from the Bulgarian folk song *Тръгнала Румяна за вода студена* [Tragnala Rumiana za voda studena].

In **"Ruschuk, Rousse, on the Danube"** the old and the new name of the city of birth of Elias Canetti are both in the title. Elias Canetti (1905 – 1994) was a modernist author who won the Nobel Prize in Literature in 1981 "for writings marked by a broad outlook, a wealth of ideas and artistic power." He was a German-language writer born in Bulgaria and a British citizen.

Ecoglasnost was the strong anti-dictatorship opposition in Bulgaria which made political changes in 1989. This movement started because of the illnesses of the people in Rousse due to air pollution from a factory on the Romanian side of the Danube and the government's failure to take action to correct the situation.

Gertrude Stein (1874 – 1946) was an American novelist, poet, playwright, and art collector who hosted a Paris salon where the leading figures of modernism in literature and art met. She was one of the first to write about how a view from an airplane changes human perception of the world.

"Forwarded Greetings" is dedicated to Konstantin Pavlov and was written in Bulgarian on the day he passed away. His poems, as well as Vutimski's, were, for me, a window outside the "official poetry" under the dictatorship. In this volume, I include my English translation of the German poem-clone from 2009 because the Bulgarian poem includes more figures and themes that, in my eyes, overly complicate the translated poem for a Western reader.

Konstantin Pavlov (1933 –2008), a poet and screenwriter, was among the few Bulgarian intellectuals who dared to act autonomously and defy the Bulgarian Communist government, which ruled the country from 1945 until 1989. Government censors began a ten-year-long publishing ban against his work beginning in 1966, but Bulgarians began illegally publishing and reading his work.

Alexander Vutimski (1919 – 1943) is one of the major names of Bulgarian litereature between the two World Wars.

Ljubomir Levchev (1935 – 2019) was a Bulgarian poet and a chairman of the Bulgarian Writers' Union in the 1980s.

"The Beginning and the End of the Metaphor" is the third poem I wrote with this title. In the other-verses in German, I use the word *Seepferdchen* (English: seahorse) and in Bulgarian *водно конче* (in English: "water horse" if we take the two separate words but as a whole meaning the translation is "dragonfly"). In my first language, the poem comes from the joy of breathing the crisp air while riding a dragonfly over the water, but if you ride a seahorse you need to learn a new way of breathing, don't you? Going back to the spacetime of my English, a second language in my early childhood, the new poem is referring to the source and place of memory acquirement in the brain.

"Poetry and Philosophy of the Presence" is joyfully referring to the discussion about rhythms in poetry being related to brain activity, which I find interesting but insufficient. In my essays I develop the concept of poetry as a heritage and reservoir of knowledge, including scientific knowledge. The interpretation of the German word for poetry, *Dichtung*, as in its origins in the word "dictation," corresponds to how poetic meter was necessary for memorizing information in antiquity. However, another nuance of the word recalls the meaning "condense, full of density." After the technological breakthrough of printing, the latter fits better than meter when we consider ways of passing on knowledge. Today we include increasingly complex knowledge into the same volume of words through poetic density. New technologies of the 21st century bring even more complexity but simultaneously allow this complexity to simplify.

In **"Violet's Wayfairing"** the translation of the title refers to the combination of the two words *wayfair* and *fairytale* in the original title. Violet, a flower, and a girl called Violet inhabit the prose poem "Violas Gehschichten," so the original combines the verb *gehen* [walk, go] and the nouns *geschichten* [stories, narratives] and *schichten* [layers, stacks].

Trajectories and Latitudes

"Taking Flight" is the third poem in a series of poems written in German that vary widely in length and meaning. This series of poems is cloning while combining the "narrative method," as Eliot calls it, referring to James Joyce's *Ulysses;* Eliot's own widely-used "mythical method" and my views from String Theory. As we can read in *Quantum Poetics: Yeats, Pound, Eliot, and the Science of Modernism.*

(Cambridge University Press, 1997) by Harvard professor of litera-
ture Daniel Albright (1945 –2015), the English modernists were the
writers who deeply connected with the main ideas of the natural sci-
ences that shaped and continue to shape our era. In works of other
scholars, we can follow how Eliot and Schrödinger shared the same
understanding of simultaneity and tradition.

As a child in Western Bulgaria, I was raised with Greek epos and
Greek mythology as the most natural fairytales a grandparent would
tell. The citations from "Hymn to Aphrodite" by Sappho are from
an English translation by William Hyde Appleton in the volume *Greek
Poets in English Verse* (Cambridge: The Riverside Press, 1893).

Though "Hymn to Aphrodite" is conventionally considered to be
completely preserved, the poem's initial word is uncertain. Some
sources render it as *Ποικιλόφρον* and others as *Ποικιλόθρον*. Both are
compounds of the adjective *ποικιλος* (literally "many-colored";
metaphorically "diverse," "complex," "subtle"); *–θρον* means "chair,"
and *φρον* "mind."

The name Daedalus refers to Greek mythology and to Steven
Dedalus from *A Portrait of the Artist as a Young Man* (1916) by the mod-
ernist Irish author James Joyce (1882 – 1941), who lets his protagonist
formulate a theory of art as intelligible matter directed toward an
aesthetic end.

Ari (Asparuh) Leshnikoff (1897 – 1978) was a Bulgarian tenor in the
legendary German ensemble *Comedian Harmonists* that performed
from 1928 – 1934 as one of the most successful musical groups in
Europe One of the songs they performed was *That's the Love of the*

Sailors (1931).

The Chorus is the original soundtrack of the 2004 Academy Award-nominated French film *Les choristes* performed by The Little Singers of Saint-Marc and the Bulgarian Symphony Orchestra. In this poem I also refer to the poem "River" by the American poet Jennifer Kwon Dobbs from *Paper Pavilion* (White Pine Press, 2007) and to the song *The Downeaster Alexa*, written and performed by one of my favorite singers, Billy Joel.

"Latitudes" and **"Selected Affordable Studio Apartments"** were written in 2014. The latter is a cycle of twelve poems that can be regarded both a as a cycle and as individual poems. They were written in German and self-translated into Bulgarian and English. They are inspired by the tri-lingual work of the French-German poet Yvan Goll (1891 – 1950). Tristan Torsi, Isaac Lang, Jean de Saint-Dié, Ivan Lassang, Johannes Thor, Jean Langeville, Yvan sans Terre are pen names the poet used.

The epitaph of each poem is a quote from a poem by Yvan Goll and serves as a title. The poems are also inspired by Goll's photographs from his travels. My citations are from his collections: *Poèmes d'amour* (1930), *Love Poems in English* (1947), *Paris brennt. Ein Album nebst einem Postkartenalbum* (1921), *La Chanson de Jean sans Terre (*1936), *Fruit from Saturn* (1946), English poems (1940-1947) in his *Collected Works* in four volumes (Ed. Barbara Glauert-Hesse. Berlin: Argon, 1996).

"The Solitude of the Bee, or Correspondence with Kappus" was written in 2007 in Germany. I have used here the original title as it was created. The Austrian author Franz Xaver Kappus (1883 –

1966 was the young poet to whom Rainer Maria Rilke wrote his famous letters. Rainer Maria Rilke (1875 – 1926) was a Bohemian-Austrian poet who wrote in German and French. He is widely recognized as one of the most lyrically intense poets and considered to be a major poet of literary modernity. The epitaph of the poem is from Rilke's essay "August Rodin" (1902) and the citation in part 3 is from the poem "Poet's Death" (1892).

Three Times Daily Rhinoceros Bicornis

The poems in this section are from 2010 to 2017 and are translations from the German originals. Exceptions are the poems **"Jonah and the Cigarette Smoke,"** which was translated from the Bulgarian, and **"Sleepless,"** the first half of which was originally written in German while the second half was written in English.

"On the Shore, the Cell Harp" was written 2011 when a nuclear plant exploded after a tsunami caused by an earthquake; and with the memory of the Chernobyl nuclear disaster 1986 which I experienced as a student of atomic physics in a communist Bulgaria.

Funaoka, Fukiage, Ukishima, Fukushima are settlements in Japan. Kogarashi and Yokotate are forests described in *The Pillow Book* by Japanese poet and court lady Sei Shōnagon (c. 966 – 1017 or 1025) who served the Empress Teishi around the year 1000 during the middle Heian period.

Bikini Atoll is a coral reef in Micronesia. Its inhabitants were relocated in 1946, after which the islands and lagoon were the site of twenty-three nuclear tests conducted by the United States until 1958.

In **"Record Heat,"** #MeTwo is a hashtag that spread to the general public and the mass media from mid-2018 to draw attention to the extent of racist harassment similar to the way #MeToo stands against sexual harassment and assault.

José F.A. Oliver, to whom the poem **"Bait"** is dedicated, is a contemporary German-language poet of Spanish origin. In his experimental verse, I found the idea of intimacy as protection for the imagination.

The epitaph in **"Pledge"** is from the ballad *Die Bürgschaft* by the German poet and playwright Friedrich Schiller (1759 – 1805). The Maltese language has words that come from Arabic, such as *kbir* (large) and from Italian, such as *gravi* (serious).

The rhinoceros originated fifty million years ago. Illegal poaching for the international rhino horn trade is a major threat to their continued existence.

Antroposcene

This section includes poems from the chapbook with the same name that were written predominantly in 2000 and 2017. They explore the current epoch in which translation between national languages—but even more between points of view, frames of thinking, paradigms, and methods—is urgently needed. Multilingualism is an inherent necessity in today's literature and its innovative struggle for a language aesthetic that help us create an acceptable future together. The quest for language enables us to experience other narratives. A fully foreign word makes us stop, brings the needed frustration, and makes the urgency to make a choice and a relationship clear. One can look to fill the gaps of non-understanding or to smiply ignore them, but one needs to be aware of their existence.

Brigitte is the largest women's magazine in Germany, with a circulation of around 800,000 and an estimated readership of 3.6 million.

The chords are from the song *Once in a Lifetime* by the American rock band Taking Heads (active between 1975 – 1991), which is considered to be one of the 100 most important American musical works of the 20th century.

Wonder Detector

The poems in this section are from 2018 and 2019. Some of them use the language of high mathematics but do not demand the understanding of it. The idea of the many worlds and alternate dimensions and timelines—as well as the idea of the genetic heritage, in particular DNA and subsequently of cloning— is directly related to the legacy of Erwin Schrödinger. One of the fathers of modern natural science, he advanced these concepts in the 1950s. He was also the author of a poetry collection. I published an essay on his poems in *Science and Education* (Springer, 2013).

A *loutrophoros* is a distinctive type of Greek pottery vessel used to carry water for a bride's pre-nuptial ritual bath.

In **"Strong Interaction"** I cite in Polish from Nobel Laureate Wisława Szymborska's poem "I am too close to him to dream of me" that I read as a student because Blaga Dimitrova gave me its Bulgarian translation. Szymborska and Dimitrova were for many years friends in poetry.

Blaga Dimitrova (1922 –2003) was a Bulgarian poet and Vice President of Bulgaria from 1992 – 1993, following the establishment of a democracy. I became friends with her in 1978 through my Bulgarian literature teacher.

Dark energy is a term that describes a form of energy with unknown properties that affects our local universe on the largest scales and dominates because it is uniform across space. Together with *dark matter* it contributes 95% of the total energy in the present-day observable universe. In *Homo Ludens* (1938) Dutch historian Johan Huizinga (1892 – 1945) discusses the importance of the element of play to culture and society. The Latin word *ludens* has no direct equivalent in English, as it simultaneously refers to sport, play, school, and practice.

In **"Set of Possibilities,"** Schrödinger's cat is a thought-experiment by the Nobel Prize-winning Austrian physicist Erwin Schrödinger (1887 – 1961) who developed a number of fundamental theories in quantum physics. The Schrödinger equation provides a way to calculate the wave function of a system and how it changes dynamically in time. In addition, he was the author of many works on various aspects of the natural sciences. He also wrote about theoretical biology and in his book *What is Life?* addressed the problems of genetics. He paid great attention to the philosophical aspects of science, ancient and oriental philosophical concepts, ethics, religion, poetry and translation.

Original Sources

Reflections in a Well. With Rumiana Ebert. London: Paekakariki Press, 2019.

A föld színe. (The Color of the Earth). Selected poems, short stories, essays, interviews and texts for theater. Ed. Johanna Domokos. Hungarian translations: Viktória Csörgo, Ildikó Kovács, Klaudia Katzenbach. Budapest: L'Harmattan, 2018.

Прегърнати от мълата (Embraced by the fog). Edition Завръщания. Sofia: Fo, 2018.

Anthroposzene. (Anthroposcene). Edition Translingual. Bielefeld: Hochroth, 2017.

selected affordable studio apartments. German, Bulgarian and English by the poet. French translation: Jean Portante. English editor: Chantal Wright. Photographs: Yvan Goll. Berlin: Hochroth, 2015.

Landschaften, Ufer. (Landscapes, shore) Edition Lyrik Kabinett. München: Hanser, 2013.

La Solitute de L'Abeille/ Die Einsamkeit der Biene. (The Solitude of the Bee) French and German. Translation into French by Jean Portante. Paris: Éditions L'Oreille du Loup, 2013.

A Hand full of Water / Eine Hand voll Wasser. Enlarged edition. English Translation: Chantal Wright. Buffalo, New York: White Pine Press, 2012.

Viadukte. (Viaducts) Poetry and Art Book. Images by Johannes Häfner. Nürnberg: ICHverlag Häfner & Häfner, 2010.

Diese Stadt kann auch weiß sein. (The city may also be snowy). Short stories and prose poems. Berlin: Hans Schiler Verlag, 2010.

Drei Frauen. (Three Women). German, Finish, Bulgarian. With Sabine Kleinert and Orvokki Vääriskoski. Translation into Finish by Orvokki Vääriskoski. Leipzig: Engelsdorfer Verlag, 2009.

Eine Hand voll Wasser. (A Handful of Water). Edition Zeitzeichen. Aschersleben: Un Art Ig, 2008.

Завръщането на белия бик (The Return of the White Bull). Plovdiv: Zhanet45, 2007.

Разпознавания (Discernments/Recognitions). Plovdiv: Zhanet45, 2006.

Gefangen im Licht. (Captured in Light). Bulgarian and German. With translations by Gaby Tiemann and the author. Marburg an der Lahn: Biblion, 1999.

Зачеваща памет (Conceiving Memory). Edition Avantgarde. Bulgarian. Sofia: Prosoretz, 1994.

Chicago Blues. Bilingual. Bulgarian and English by the poet. Sofia: SPO 1992.

As well as in the journals *Младеж* (1/1988), *transkrit* (2/2010), *Das Gedicht* (27/2019), *Spiegelungen* (1/2019) and the anthology *All dies hier,*

Acknowledgments

I am very thankful to poet and publisher Dennis Maloney for the opportunity to present my poetics in this volume and am deeply touched by his understanding of my work. I am delighted to have had as editor Jennifer Kwon Dobbs, whose poetry I highly appreciate, and thank her for her loving dedication to this book, reading a large number of poems from different periods and inspiring and supporting me in all steps during my work on the manuscript. I thank Chantal Wright for her new translations in this volume, and I am very grateful to her for being on my side in many different ways in my work in adopted languages for many years. I cannot miss thanking also Mária Chilf for the image on this book cover and Elaine LaMattina from White Pine Press who developed the book's design.

I thank all poets whom I have read for their existence and all my readers for their interest and reciprocal inspiration.

My parents brought me to a multiverse, and I am sure that my father would have been happy to hold this book in his hands. I thank my mother for her love and patience always and also while I was working on the manuscript. I thank my beloved man who lives with me in the multiverse unconditionally and our daughter, who not only brought a multiverse into my life but let me see the one inside myself.

I feel fortunate to exist in the same time and the same space and to share the energy of poetry with you all.

Biographies

TZVETA SOFRONIEVA is the author of collections of poetry, short stories, essays, theatre texts, articles, translations and literary art installations. Her works have been published and awarded in many countries. She is the editor of poetry anthologies and intercultural collections, including *Verbotene Worte* [Forbidden Words] (Biblion, Munich, 2005), *11.9. Web Streaming Poetry* (Belgrade 2010) and *Космоси* [Cosmos] (Fo, Sofia, since 2018) and curates readings series, including *Wissen der Dichtung* [The Knowledge of Poetry] (House of Poetry, Berlin, 2015) and *mehrsprachig ringen* [together in multilingualism] (Lettrétage, Berlin, 2019). Born in Sofia, Bulgaria, she has made Berlin her home since 1992.

JENNIFER KWON DOBBS, born in Wonju, Republic of Korea, is an award-winning American poet and the author of two books of poetry and two chapbooks, most recently *Interrogation Room* (White Pine Press 2018), mentioned in *The New York Times* and praised by *World Literature Today,* and *Necro Citizens* edited by Johanna Domokos (translingual series, hochroth Bielefeld, German and English edition, 2019). She is also co-editor of *Radical Kinships: An Autocritical Anthology* (Demeter Press forthcoming) and poetry editor of *AGNI,* published by Boston University. Currently an associate professor of creative writing and program director of Race and Ethnic Studies at St. Olaf College, she lives in Saint Paul, Minnesota, and divides her time among her families in Hamburg and Seoul.

CHANTAL WRIGHT is an Associate Professor at the University of Warwick in the U.K. She is the author of *Literary Translation'* (Routledge, 2016) and the translator of Antoine Berman's *The Age of Translation* (Routledge, 2018). She received an award from PEN American Center's translation fund to translate Tzveta Sofronieva's collection of poetry *A Hand Full of Water,* which was subsequently awarded the inaugural Cliff Becker Book Prize in Translation in 2012.

MÁRIA CHILF studied painting at the Hungarian Academy of Fine Arts and completed her training at the Hochschule der Künste in Berlin. Her installations, graphics and aquarelles were exhibited in New York City in 2001 and in many places in Europe. Born in Tirgu Mures, Romania, she has lived in Budapest since the 1990s. Her images have graced the covers of Tzveta Sofronieva's books since 1996 when the artist and the poet met as fellows of the Academy Schloss Solitude in Stuttgart.